KAMPFGRUPPE PEIPER

KAMPFGRUPPE PEIPER

The Race for the Meuse

David Cooke and Wayne Evans

Pen & Sword
MILITARY

First published in Great Britain in 2005
Paperback edition 2014 by Pen & Sword Military
an imprint of
Pen & Sword Books Ltd
47 Church Street
Barnsley
South Yorkshire
S70 2AS

Copyright © David Cooke and Wayne Evans 2005, 2014

ISBN 978 1 47382 704 2

Typeset in Palatino by
Mac Style Ltd, Bridlington, East Yorkshire
Printed and bound in the UK by CPI Group (UK) Ltd,
Croydon, CR0 4YY

Pen & Sword Books Ltd incorporates the imprints of Pen &
Sword Archaeology, Atlas, Aviation, Battleground, Discovery,
Family History, History, Maritime, Military, Naval, Politics,
Railways, Select, Transport, True Crime, and Fiction,
Frontline Books, Leo Cooper, Praetorian Press, Seaforth
Publishing and Wharncliffe.

For a complete list of Pen & Sword titles please contact
PEN & SWORD BOOKS LIMITED
47 Church Street, Barnsley, South Yorkshire,
S70 2AS, England
E-mail: enquiries@pen-and-sword.co.uk
Website: www.pen-and-sword.co.uk

CONTENTS

Preface

The Ardennes offensive in December 1944 was Adolf Hitler's last throw of the dice. A huge German force struck the thin American lines in the Ardennes, in Belgium, bursting through and driving on for the River Meuse, with the objective of reaching Antwerp and cutting off a major part of the Allied forces from their supply sources. Although many histories of the battle look at the whole offensive in terms of corps, divisions and regiments, the fighting took place at a much lower level. Many of the actions fought across the whole front were at the company or battalion level. In these actions small groups of men, and even individuals, were instrumental in winning or losing the battle. This holds true for the fighting that Kampfgruppe Peiper was involved in.

Obersturmbannführer Jochen Peiper commanded the spearpoint unit of the German offensive, with the objective of seizing one or more crossings of the Meuse. Peiper and his American opponents fought a series of fascinating actions over a period of eight days, and these are covered in detail using the accounts of the participants and after-action reports of the units involved. The fighting became very confused, with elements of both sides vying for possession of a number of towns and villages, and other units being drawn into the fighting. It is the objective of this book to detail each day's fighting, area by area, and with the use of numerous maps give a clear, concise description of the action.

Glossary

AAA	Anti-aircraft Artillery
CCB	Combat Command B
CP	Command Post
ECB	Engineer Combat Battalion
IR	Infantry Regiment
I & R	Intelligence and Reconnaissance
Kampfgruppe (KG)	Battle group
Nebelwerfer	Multi-barrelled rocket launcher
Panzerfaust	German one-shot infantry anti-tank weapon
PIR	Parachute Infantry Regiment
Pz.AA.1	Panzer Aufklarungs Abteilung 1 (Panzer Reconnaissance Battalion 1)
Pz.Rgt 1	Panzer Regiment 1
Pz.Gren.Rgt 1	Panzergrenadier Regiment 1
Pz.Gren.Rgt 2	Panzergrenadier Regiment 2
Rollbahn	March route
Schwimmwagen	German amphibious jeep
Spitze	Advance guard
Spitzen Company	Advance guard company. Followed behind the *spitze* and provided support for them.
SPW	Schutzenpanzerwagen. Variants of the SdKfz 251 half-track. Used for carrying infantry and engineers, and as mortar- and weapon-carriers.
TAC	Tactical Air Command
TB	Tank Battalion
TF	Task Force
VG	Volksgrenadier
TD	Tank destroyer. Either a towed or self-propelled anti-tank gun.

Peiper at Westphalia during reorganisation of his Panzer regiment prior to
Operation 'Wacht am Rhein' November 1944.

Chapter One

WACHT AM RHEIN

Operation *Wacht am Rhein* (Watch on the Rhine), in December 1944, was Hitler's last great offensive in the west. His plan was to cut a swathe through the Ardennes, cross the Meuse and drive on to Antwerp, thus cutting off the British 21st Army Group and the American 9th Army from their supply sources. This, it was hoped, would lead to mass surrender or a second Dunkirk. Following such a major disaster the Allies would be forced to sue for peace. Then Hitler could turn his whole attention on the Soviets.

By December 1944 the Allies had driven the German forces back to the West Wall, Germany's equivalent of the French Maginot Line. The breakout from Normandy, in August 1944, was followed by a rapid pursuit of the disorganized German forces across France and into Belgium. By early September the Allied advance was in danger of grinding to a halt, not because

Hitler plans a shock for the Allies in the west.

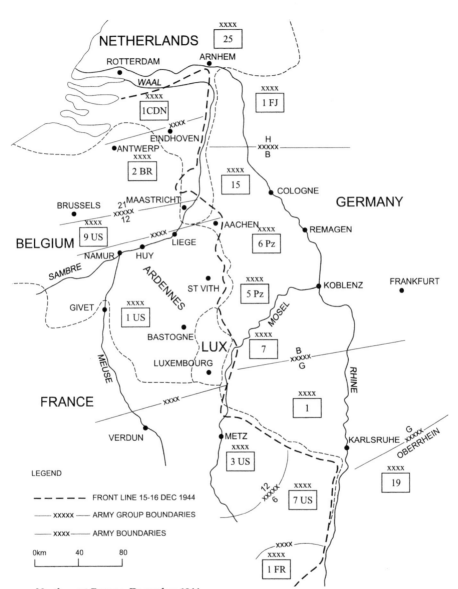

North-west Europe, December 1944.

of German resistance, but a shortage of supplies. Most of the Allied supplies were still coming over the Normandy beaches or through a number of small ports the Allies had captured intact. Cherbourg, a major port captured early in the campaign, had all its facilities destroyed by the German garrison before

The planned objective of the Ardennes offensive.

it surrendered, and was in the process of being repaired. Antwerp, in Belgium, another major port, had been captured by the British with its docks in full working order. Unfortunately, its approaches along the Scheldt Estuary were still held by the Germans, so shipping was unable to reach the port.

The Allied High Command was in a quandary. Eisenhower wanted to continue advancing on a broad front, but the supply situation would not allow this without a pause to build up resources. Montgomery put forward a plan for a single thrust to cross the Rhine at Arnhem and drive on into the Ruhr. This led to Operation *Market-Garden*, the largest airborne operation of the war. With *Market-Garden's* failure to capture the road bridge at Arnhem, Eisenhower reverted to the broad-front strategy.

North of the Ardennes lies the Huertgen Forest. American forces attacked the Germans entrenched in its inhospitable terrain, which the autumn rains had turned into a quagmire. Several American divisions were severely mauled before the battle ground to a halt. The Allies continued to push against the West Wall, but made little progress.

The Ardennes was a quiet sector of the front, and little movement had taken place for several months. It was so quiet that the Americans used it as a rest zone for divisions that had been battered in the fighting in the Huertgen Forest, and as a quiet area to introduce fresh divisions, newly arrived from the United States, to the rigours of the front line. This meant that the German offensive would face two worn divisions, with many new replacements, and two completely untried divisions, with inexperienced commanders. The Germans were aware of this and kept the area quiet, with little active patrolling and a minimum of artillery fire, and succeeded in lulling the Allied commanders into a false sense of security.

With this in mind, *Wacht am Rhein* was planned under the greatest secrecy. Even its name, Watch on the Rhine, gave the idea of a purely defensive operation. Very few people, including many senior officers, were informed about it until a few days before the offensive was to begin, and all communications were made by hand. Mention of the operation in radio or telephone communications was strictly forbidden and any transgressions of this order were to be dealt with most severely. This meant that the Allies' main source of intelligence about German intentions, Ultra, was useless. 'Ultra' was the codename for the radio interception and codebreaking work done at Bletchley Park, in Buckinghamshire, the source of which was known to only the most senior Allied commanders. Some senior German commanders argued against the scope of the offensive and suggested a 'small solution', which entailed a much more limited offensive breaking through the Allied lines in two places and forming a pocket. Hitler would have none of it. He wanted an all-or-nothing offensive that would win the war on the western front in one fell swoop.

Few of Hitler's commanders believed that the offensive could succeed, but by this stage of the war Hitler's plans were beyond discussion. He believed he was a great strategist and that he had saved Germany from the mistakes of many of his frontline generals. The German officer corps was living in a state of fear after the July bomb plot, in which disaffected officers had attempted to assassinate Hitler. After the round of reprisals following the plot, any disagreement was seen by Hitler as treason, and any German officer suspected of being defeatist would be dealt with swiftly, usually, in the case of senior officers, by being removed from their posts.

The attack was codenamed *Autumn Mist*. Its first wave would comprise seven panzer and thirteen infantry divisions, and these would be followed up by a further two panzer and seven infantry divisions. The whole force was divided into three armies: 5th and 6th Panzer Armies and 7th Army.

The northern flank of the offensive was formed by 6th Panzer Army, commanded by Sepp Dietrich. Dietrich's first line was formed of two corps, LXVII Corps, formed of two volksgrenadier divisions and I SS Panzer Corps with two panzer, one fallschirmjager (parachute) and two volksgrenadier divisions. In the centre was General Hasso Manteuffel's 5th Panzer Army and General Erich Brandenberger's 7th Army formed the southern flank. 6th Panzer Army would carry out the main attack, with 5th Panzer Army providing protection for its southern flank. Seventh Army would advance alongside 5th Panzer and deploy in an east-west line to protect the southern flank of the whole breakthrough.

The role of 6th Panzer Army

The initial breakthrough would be made by the four volksgrenadier divisions and one fallschirmjager division of the LXVII and I SS Panzer Corps. Once the breakthrough had been made I SS Panzer Corps' two panzer divisions – I SS Panzer Division Leibstandarte Adolf Hitler and 12th SS Panzer Division Hitler Jugend (Hitler Youth) – would push to and cross the Meuse close to Liege. Kampfgruppe Peiper would be the lead element of the Leibstandarte, and was planned to be the spearhead of the whole offensive, and the first to cross the Meuse. Once I SS Panzer Corps had achieved its objective the follow-up troops of II SS Panzer Corps – 2nd SS Panzer Division Das Reich and 9th SS Panzer Division Hohenstaufen – would exploit to the north-west and capture Antwerp. While the panzer divisions swept towards the west the infantry divisions would form an east–west line, in a similar manner to the 7th Army, to protect the northern shoulder of the breakthrough.

Oberstgruppenführer Josef (Sepp) Dietrich, commander of the 6th Panzer Army. When he commanded the Leibstandarte and I SS Panzer Corps he always sent his officers into combat with the instruction to 'bring my boys back'.

The panzer divisions would move along a number of routes (Rollbahns). The Hitler Jugend would use the most northerly of these routes, Rollbahns B and C, while the Leibstandarte would use Rollbahns D and E. Rollbahn A was an offshoot of Rollbahn B and was intended to allow forces to relieve a parachute force, which will be discussed later. It has been written in the past that the German commanders were under strict orders to stick to their assigned routes, but in reality this does not seem to have been the case. As will be seen, Obersturmbannführer Jochen Peiper switched between routes on a number of occasions, as the situation dictated. For example, his initial breakthrough was to the south of his assigned route, while his final push through La Gleize and Stoumont was on a road between two of the planned routes.

Two other operations would impact on 6th Panzer Army. A force of fallschirmjager, commanded by Colonel von der Heydte, would parachute into the area of the Baraque Michel crossroads, to the north of the main drive

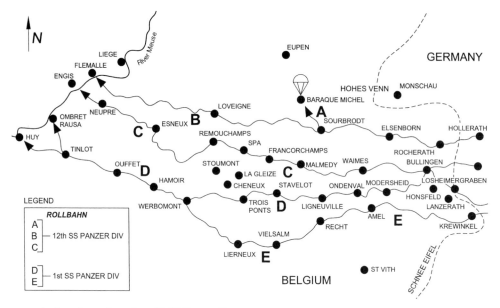

Assigned march routes of I SS Panzer Corps.

(Operation *Stoesser*). Control of the crossroads would seriously impede the movement of American reinforcements into the area. The paratroopers would be quickly relieved by elements of the Hitler Jugend. The other operation, *Unternehmen Greif*, was under the command of Otto Skorzeny, a special-operations expert. Skorzeny had recruited a number of English-speaking soldiers, who had been equipped with American uniforms and equipment. Divided into small groups of three or four men, and transported in a captured jeep, they would drive in front of the main German advance causing chaos and confusion by interfering with traffic signs and spreading false information to the American troops they encountered. It was even planned that they could assist in the capture of a bridge once the Meuse had been reached. It is beyond the scope of this book to discuss the events surrounding these operations in any detail, but neither of them achieved the desired results.

The Leibstandarte was commanded by Oberführer Wilhelm Mohnke, a veteran officer who had served throughout the war in both the Leibstandarte and the Hitler Jugend divisions. He decided to divide his division into four separate battlegroups (kampfgruppen – KG). Each kampfgruppe took the name of its respective commander. Kampfgruppe Peiper, the subject of this book, was based around the 1st SS Panzer Regiment (Pz.Rgt 1) and was commanded by Obersturmbannführer Jochen Peiper. Kampfgruppe Hansen was formed from the three battalions of the 1st SS Panzergrenadier Regiment (Pz.Gren.Rgt 1), whereas Kampfgruppe Sandig comprised two battalions of the 2nd SS Panzergrenadier Regiment (Pz.Gren.Rgt 2). Sandig's other battalion was attached to Kampfgruppe Peiper. The two kampfgruppe were commanded by Obersturmbannführer Max Hansen and Sturmbannführer Rudi Sandig respectively. The final kampfgruppe was formed around Sturmbannführer Gustav Knittel's 1st SS Panzer Reconnaissance Battalion (Panzer Aufklarungs Abteilung, or Pz.AA.1). Each kampfgruppe had divisional troops such as anti-aircraft and engineers attached to them. The organization of each kampfgruppe will be discussed in the next chapter.

Peiper would lead the advance along Rollbahn C, supported by Rudi Sandig. On the more southerly Rollbahn D, Kampfgruppe Hansen would lead the way, followed closely by Schnellgruppe Knittel. Knittel had orders to switch between routes as he saw fit, to exploit the speed of his armoured cars and half-tracks (Schutzen-panzerwagens, or SPWs).

The terrain through which the German offensive was to take place was mainly heavily wooded hills divided by swift-running rivers. It was far from ideal, with mechanized forces mainly restricted to the roads, some of which are difficult to negotiate in a car, let alone a King Tiger. That said, it had been the starting point

Oberführer Wilhelm Mohnke commanded the 1st SS Panzer Division *Leibstandarte Adolf Hitler.*

for the highly successful German offensive against France in 1940, when German panzer forces had surprised the French with their appearance at Sedan after crossing the 'impassable' terrain of the Ardennes. It was for exactly this reason that the Americans used the Ardennes as a rest and recuperation area for divisions that had been battered in the fighting in the Huertgen Forest. It was also used as a gentle introduction to frontline life for inexperienced divisions, such as the 106th Division, which had recently arrived in Europe and had yet to receive its baptism of fire. Defending the line in front of the 6th Panzer Army was the 99th Division, another new division, with its three regiments. To its south was the 106th Division deployed on the Schnee Eifel. There was a 5-kilometre gap between the two divisions, the Losheim Gap, which was covered by only a single cavalry squadron, the 18th, based around Manderfeld. This gap was a major weakness in the American line and would be exploited by the German attack.

Due to the secrecy of the operation, orders were not issued until very close to the event. Sepp Dietrich was not briefed on 6th Panzer Army's role until 29 November. Divisional commanders were then given their orders on 6

December, with a subsequent briefing by Hitler at the Adlerhof on the 11th. It was not until 11:00 hrs on the 14th that Mohnke briefed his senior officers, less than forty-eight hours before the offensive began. Peiper held an orders group at his headquarters in the Forsthaus Blankheimer Wald on his return from divisional headquarters on the afternoon of the 14th.

The offensive was due to start at 05:30 hrs on 16 December. The members of the kampfgruppe had moved into their deployment area in the Blankenheimer Wald on the 12th, two days before Peiper had been given his orders. Although the Americans were aware, from a number of small hints, that something was afoot, they were taken completely by surprise when the German barrage opened.

The effects on the civilian population

Many civilians were caught up in the offensive. In many of the towns and villages behind the American front line, life had almost returned to normal, and many people prepared to celebrate their first Christmas of freedom, after four years of German occupation. The offensive struck with such speed that many civilians had no time to evacuate the area. The inhabitants of many of the villages and towns fought over by KG Peiper were still in place when the Germans arrived. Neither side had any qualms about bombarding urban areas occupied by their opposition, and the civilians had to take their chances along with the combatants, sheltering in cellars with the wounded. There were many civilian casualties, some from artillery and small-arms fire, but others seem to have been deliberately killed, and a number of both German and American accounts talk of civilians been executed by members of the kampfgruppe. This does not seem to have been a deliberate policy, but the act of individuals, as were the shootings of American prisoners.

When the civilians emerged from their cellars after the fighting had moved on they found a scene of desolation. Most of the houses were reduced to rubble, or at best badly damaged, and few buildings survived the battle intact. Many villages that had been bypassed by the Germans, or passed through with little fighting during the early stages of the offensive, suffered a similar fate when the Americans pushed the Germans back to their start line during January 1945. It was a scene repeated across north-west Europe, wherever a town or village was fought over, from Normandy to the Elbe. It would take many years for the civilian population to rebuild their shattered lives.

Chapter Two

KAMPFGRUPPE PEIPER: ORGANIZATION AND EQUIPMENT

Obersturmbannführer Jochen Peiper commanded Panzer Regiment 1 of the 1st SS Panzer Division Leibstandarte and it was around this unit that the kampfgruppe was formed. Peiper had a number of other elements from the division and I SS Panzer Corps attached to the kampfgruppe, and each will be discussed below.

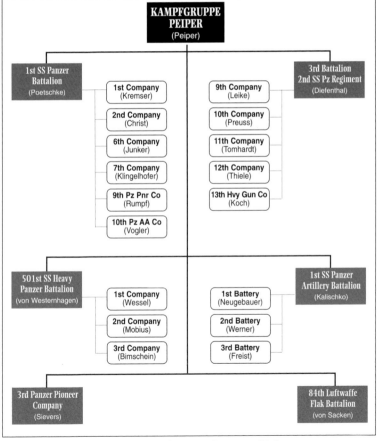

Organization of Kampfgruppe Peiper.

1st SS Panzer Battalion
(Sturmbannführer Werner Poetschke)
Panzer Regiment 1 should normally have had two battalions, the first equipped with Panthers and the second with Mk IVs. Due to a lack of equipment a composite battalion had been formed, with two companies (1 and 2) of Panthers and two companies (6 and 7) of Mk IVs.

3rd SS (SPW) Panzergrenadier Battalion
(Hauptsturmführer Jupp Diefenthal)
On paper this unit was part of Rudi Sandig's Panzergrenadier Regiment 2, but in practice almost always formed part of the panzergruppe with Panzer Regiment 1. It was the only battalion in the division that was carried in half-tracks (SPWs), all the other panzergrenadier battalions moving on foot or by lorry. The battalion had five companies – three rifle companies (9, 10 and 11), a heavy weapons company (12) and a heavy-infantry-gun company (13).

501st SS Heavy Panzer Battalion
(Obersturmbannführer Hein von Westernhagen)
The 501st was not a divisional unit, but was part of the I SS Panzer Corps. It was attached to Peiper to compensate for the missing battalion of Panzer Regiment 1. On paper the battalion's three companies should have had a total of forty-five King Tigers between them. In reality, due to the unreliability of the King Tiger, it never achieved anything like this number in combat at any given time.

1st Panzer Artillery Battalion
(Hauptsturmführer Ludwig Kalischko)
For artillery support Peiper had attached the 1st Battalion of Panzer Artillery Regiment 1. The battalion's three batteries should have been equipped with the self-propelled 105mm howitzer known as the Wespe. Once again, due to the lack of available equipment, the unit had to make do with what was available and each battery was equipped with six towed 105mm guns.

9th SS Panzer Pioneer Company
(Hauptsturmführer Erich Rumpf)
This company was an integral part of Panzer Regiment 1 and provided engineer support for the regiment. The bulk of the company was equipped with SPWs.

3rd SS Panzer Pioneer Company
(Obersturmführer Franz Sievers)
This company was nominally part of the divisional pioneer battalion, but invariably formed part of the Panzergruppe. The company had two platoons in SPWs and two in lorries.

JOCHEN PEIPER

Born on 30 January 1915 in the Wilmersdorf district in Berlin, Peiper joined the SS-Reiter (Cavalry) in October 1933 for voluntary service. He was selected for SS NCO training at Juterborg in January 1935, and then promoted to Untersturmführer on 20 April 1936 and posted to 3rd Battalion, Leibstandarte SS Adolf Hitler. In 1938, on promotion to Obersturmführer, Peiper was seconded to the staff of SS-Reichsführer Heinrich Himmler as a liaison officer. Peiper rejoined the Leibstandarte as a company commander in May 1940 during the attack on France, winning the Iron Cross 1st and 2nd Class and promotion to Hauptsturmführer.

By November 1940 Peiper was back on Himmler's staff as his adjutant. He remained at Himmler's side until August 1941 when he rejoined the Leibstandarte, which was then heavily engaged in southern Russia. In January 1943 the Leibstandarte fought at Kharkov, during which time Peiper was promoted Sturmbannführer, and was awarded the Knight's Cross and the German Cross in gold. Peiper fought in Russia until July 1943, alongside others who would be with him in the Ardennes – Max Hansen, Rudi Sandig, Werner Poetschke and Hein von Westernhagen.

The Leibstandarte was transferred to northern Italy for rest and refitting (twenty-five years later, Peiper and two other officers were accused of war crimes in Boves by an Italian court). By November the division was back in southern Russia where Peiper was awarded the Oakleaves to his Knight's Cross, earned by his leadership in action near Zhitomir. The Leibstandarte suffered terrible casualties during the winter fighting in Russia and was transferred to Belgium in April 1944 to rebuild. By this time Peiper had been promoted Obersturmbannführer and given command of Panzer Regiment 1.

Obersturmbannführer Jochen Peiper, commander of 1st Panzer Regiment of the Leibstandarte.

Peiper was wounded during the Normandy campaign and did not rejoin the division until October 1944, when the division was again rebuilding after suffering heavy losses during the Normandy campaign. He commanded Kampfgruppe Peiper during the Ardennes offensive, after which the remnants of the kampfgruppe, less its commander, fought around Bastogne. It is thought that Peiper at this time was suffering a breakdown from the stress of the fighting and subsequent breakout. Peiper did not return to the division until February 1945, as a Standartenführer with the Swords to his Knight's Cross. The Leibstandarte took part in German offensive around Lake Balaton, in Hungary, to relieve the garrison at Budapest, but again the division suffered grievously.

On 8 May 1945 the division was ordered to destroy its vehicles and march west into captivity. By August Peiper and other members of the kampfgruppe were on trial, charged with committing war crimes during the Ardennes fighting. He was originally sentenced to death by hanging, but this was later commuted and he was released from prison in 1956. After working in Germany, Peiper retired with his wife to live in Traves in France in 1972, where he was murdered by French Communists in 1976.

10th SS Panzer Flak Company
(Obersturmführer Karl-Heinz Vogler)

The 10th Flak Company was part of Panzer Regiment 1 and provided anti-aircraft cover for the panzers. Its three platoons were equipped with a variety of equipment – one platoon had four self-propelled 37mm anti-aircraft guns, another had four self-propelled 20mm guns and the third three Wirbelwinds, a quad 20mm gun mounted on a Mk IV chassis.

84th Luftwaffe Flak Battalion
(Major von Sacken)

Peiper had elements of von Sacken's battalion attached to provide additional anti-aircraft cover. It is difficult to establish exactly what this battalion was equipped with and how much of the battalion was present. It is likely that the battalion was equipped with a mixture of 20mm and 37mm anti-aircraft guns.

SS Panzer Supply Company
(Sturmbannführer Unger)

Unger's company provided a limited supply column for the kampfgruppe.

SS Panzer Repair Company
(Obersturmführer Ratschko)

The Panzer Repair Company provided the kampfgruppe with limited facilities to carry out running repairs on its vehicles.

Kampfgruppe Peiper was the most powerful German unit in the Ardennes offensive. It had 117 tanks, 149 SPWs, eighteen 105mm guns, six 150mm guns and over thirty anti-aircraft weapons. The unit comprised 4,800 men and 800 vehicles.

The opposition

Peiper's main opponent would be the American 30th Infantry Division, so it is worth pausing to consider its organization. An American infantry division was formed from three infantry regiments and supporting troops. In the case of the 30th, the three regiments were the 117th, 119th and 120th. Each regiment was in turn made up of three battalions, a cannon company and an anti-tank company. Each battalion was formed of three rifle companies, a weapons company and a headquarters company. Each company was lettered consecutively, so, for example, the 1st Battalion would have Companies A to D, while the 2nd Battalion had E through H, and so on.

The 30th Division also had a powerful artillery component – three battalions of twelve 105mm howitzers (118th, 197th and 230th Field Artillery Battalions) and one battalion of twelve 155mm guns (113th Field Artillery Battalion). All these guns were towed. In addition to the artillery it had two other 'fighting' units. The 30th Cavalry Recce Troop gave the division an

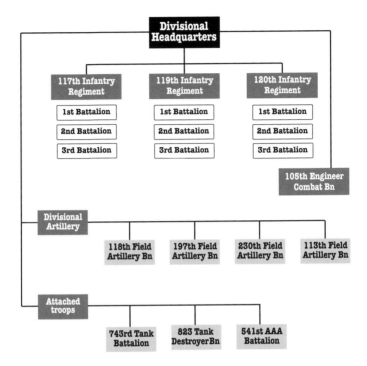

Organization of 30th US Infantry Division.

integral reconnaissance capability, while the 105th Engineer Combat Battalion (ECB) provided engineering support.

American divisions usually had a number of independent units attached to them. In the case of the 30th Infantry Division in the Ardennes, the 743rd Tank Battalion provided armoured support with its fifty-three Sherman medium tanks and seventeen Stuart light tanks, along with its integral Recce, Assault Gun and Mortar Platoons. To provide additional anti-tank capability the 823rd Tank Destroyer Battalion had twenty-four towed 3-inch anti-tank guns and twelve M-10 tank destroyers, as well as two recce platoons. Finally, the 541st Anti-aircraft Artillery (AAA) Battalion, with thirty-two 40mm anti-aircraft guns, supplied the division with anti-aircraft cover.

As will be seen, elements of other units were attached to the 30th during the course of the fighting. Combat Command B (CCB) of 3rd Armoured Division came under command of General Leland Hobbs, commanding 30th Division, during the course of the fighting around Stavelot and La Gleize. Its three task forces, McGeorge, Lovelady and Jordan, played a vital part in the fighting, as did Captain Berry's Company of the 740th Tank Battalion.

Weapons and tactics

The Germans had a major qualitative advantage over the Americans when it came to armour. The German tanks – the King Tiger, Panther and Mark IV – had both weapon and armour advantages over the Sherman. Although the Sherman could hold its own against the Mk IV, it stood little chance against a Tiger or Panther in open ground. The 88mm and 75mm guns mounted on the Tiger and Panther respectively were capable of penetrating a Sherman's armour at 2,000 metres, while the Sherman's short 75mm gun was incapable of penetrating the armour of either German tank at more than 500 metres, and then it took a lucky shot to penetrate the thick frontal armour of the panzers. The Americans had begun to introduce upgraded versions of the Sherman with thicker armour and the 76mm (3-inch) gun, and although this improved matters, the Germans still had the advantage, and many American tanks were still of the older variety.

The Americans were equipped with a number of anti-tank guns. The standard gun used in an infantry division was still the 57mm anti-tank gun. This had little chance of penetrating a German panzer at anything but close range or with a flank shot. The 3-inch anti-tank gun, both in its towed form and mounted as a self-propelled gun, the M-10, performed better. The best gun available to the Americans was the 90mm, mounted in the M-36 Tank Destroyer. Few of these were available, and only one is recorded as having fought against KG Peiper, and that was part of Captain Berry's 'mix-and-match' tank company, which had been equipped with whatever was available in the rush to block Peiper's advance.

Although the Americans had the inferior weapons systems in the tank and anti-tank battle, the terrain and weather went some way towards counteracting this. Many of the actions were fought at a few hundred yards range, due to the adverse conditions: heavy mist had been recorded on a number of days during the fighting. Scoring a hit often depended on firing the first shot, and when the range was as short as fifty yards, the German advantage was nullified. Some German tanks were susceptible to gun or gunnery system damage, particularly the Tigers. In one incident two Tigers took on a company of over fifteen Shermans at a range of 1,500 metres. The Tigers should have savaged the Shermans, but the Americans put down such a weight of fire that within a few minutes both German tanks were out of action. One tank's gunnery system had been damaged by the impact of an American round, and the other had part of its gun barrel blown off by a direct hit. Neither tank had been penetrated, but both were rendered incapable of firing, and hence were not much use to the Germans.

The Germans also had the advantage in infantry weapons and tactics. A German squad was based around its machine gun, or guns, with the rest of the squad carrying ammunition and defending the gun. The German machine gun used was the MG42, a superb weapon with a staggering rate of

PzKfw IV Ausf. H

Panzerkampfwagen Mk IV, the workhorse of the German armed forces.

Crew:	5
Weight:	23 tons
Speed:	25 mph
Main gun:	75mm KwK 40 L48
Machine guns:	2 x 7.92mm MG
Maximum armour:	50mm

The Mk IV was the workhorse of the German armoured forces and served throughout the war in various guises. It was initially equipped with a short 75mm gun, which had limited effectiveness against armour. In 1942 the F2 version of the Mk IV had been upgraded with a long 75mm gun, which gave it a vastly improved anti-tank capability. By 1944 the H and J versions were in service. These both had additional armour around the turret and side skirts, which gave much better protection to the crews.

One battalion of each panzer regiment was equipped with Mk IVs, although Kampfgruppe Peiper had only two companies, 6 and 7, which formed a single composite battalion with two companies of Panthers, 1 and 2. Most of the kampfgruppe's Mk IVs became stranded south of the Ambleve when they ran out of fuel, although the remaining fuel was siphoned into several tanks to allow them to follow the main body.

A3 M4 Sherman

A Sherman doubles as a troop transport during the fighting in Europe.
Airborne Forces Museum

Crew:	5
Weight:	32 tons
Speed:	25 mph
Main gun:	75mm or 76mm
Machine guns:	1 x .50-cal MG, x .30-cal MG
Maximum armour:	50mm

The Sherman tank was the mainstay of the Allied forces throughout the campaign in north-west Europe. Compared to its main opponents, the Tiger and Panther, it was outgunned and under-armoured, although it could hold its own against the Mk IV. The Sherman's 75mm gun had little chance of penetrating a Tiger or Panther except at point-blank range. Later versions of the Sherman were upgunned with a 76mm (3-inch) gun, which gave better penetration, but still lacked the punch of the German long 75mm and 88mm guns mounted on the Panther and King Tiger respectively. One advantage the Sherman did have was its reliability. It was produced in very large numbers, and continued in service until well after the end of the Second World War.

Sherman tanks operated in support of the 30th Infantry Division throughout its actions against Kampfgruppe Peiper. The 30th had one complete independent tank battalion attached to it, the 743rd Tank Battalion, and part of a second, the 740th. For much of the fighting, Combat Command B of the 3rd Armoured Division, with its Shermans, M5 light tanks and armoured infantry, was attached to the 30th.

fire of 1,200 rounds per minute. It could be used as either a bipod-mounted squad weapon or a tripod-mounted heavy machine gun. On the other hand, the American squad's most important element was its riflemen, armed with the semi-automatic M1 rifle. The machine guns, either Browning Automatic Rifles (BAR) or .30-calibre tripod-mounted, were used in support of the riflemen.

Above: German MG42.

Right: American Browning Automatic Rifle (BAR).

Opposite: Garand M1, standard US service rifle.

Whereas the American infantrymen in the 30th Division moved mainly on foot, or were transported by lorry, most of Peiper's men were mounted in SPWs. The SdKfz 251 was a very versatile vehicle, numerous variants operated as infantry-carriers, command vehicles, mortar-carriers, support vehicles equipped with a variety of guns, engineer vehicles, anti-aircraft vehicles, and in other roles. Jupp Diefenthal's battalion was completely equipped with an assortment of these vehicles, as were the bulk of the two engineer companies. Infantry mounted in SPWs gained the advantage of increased mobility, and each SPW had two machine guns mounted on it, to give the squad additional firepower.

One area in which the Americans had a significant advantage was artillery, both in numbers of guns and their capability. Once the Germans had been brought to a halt the Americans were able to bring a crushing amount of firepower to bear, not just with guns belonging to the divisions, but corps- and army-level assets. The Germans had fewer guns but had large numbers of mortars and nebelwerfers – multi-barrelled rocket launchers – known to the Allies as 'Moaning Minnies' because of the noise their shells made. The Germans were adept at their use – some estimates attributed up to 80 per cent of Allied casualties in the Normandy campaign to mortar and nebelwerfer fire.

In the Ardennes the Allies had control of the air above the battlefield, although bad weather meant that this had very little impact on the fighting. On the few occasions American fighter-bombers were able to intervene they caused both losses and delays to the kampfgruppe. The Americans also tried to use medium bombers as a tactical weapon, although on the one occasion this was attempted against Kampfgruppe Peiper it went badly wrong; the bombers made a mistake and released their load over a town that was occupied by American troops.

M-10A1 Tank Destroyer

The crew of this M-10 have attached spare bogie wheels and sections of tank trank to the hull, along with sandbags, as extra protection against armour-piercing shells.

Crew:	5
Weight:	28 tons
Speed:	30 mph
Main gun:	76mm M7
Machine guns:	2 x .50-cal MG
Maximum armour:	50mm

The M-10 tank destroyer was designed to provide mobile anti-tank support for American units. It first saw action in North Africa in 1942 and continued in service until the end of the hostilities. The 76mm (3-inch) gun on the M-10 was capable of penetrating 100mm at 1,000 yards. The vehicle's main drawback was its open-topped turret, which made it particularly susceptible to artillery fire. To counteract this problem some units fabricated armoured covers for the turrets.

During the Ardennes battle most American anti-tank units had a mix of M-10s and towed 3-inch anti-tank guns, both referred to as 'tank destroyers'. The US 30th Infantry Division had a number of M-10 tank destroyers in support at Stavelot, Stoumont and La Gleize.

Order of march

The lead element would be the *spitze* commanded by Obersturmführer Werner Sternebeck. This comprised a platoon of Mk IVs from 6 Company, half a platoon of Panthers from 1 Company, and a squad of pioneers from 9 Company, all from Panzer Regiment 1 (Pz.Rgt 1). Following close behind

Kampfgruppe Peiper

Order of March 16/17 December

Spitze

1 Zug, 6.Komp Pz.Rgt 1 (5 Mk IVs)

1/2 Zug/ 1.Komp Pz.Rgt 1 (2 Panthers) Obersturmführer Werner Sternebeck

1 Gruppe, 9.Komp (Pz.Pi.) Pz.Rgt 1 (SPWs)

Followed by

Spitzen Kompanie

1 Zug, 10.Komp Pz.Gren.Rgt 2

1 Zug, 9.Komp Pz.Pi. Pz.Rgt 1 (less 1 Gruppe)

1 Zug, 10.Komp Pz.Gren.Rgt 2 Hauptsturmführer Georg Preuss

1 Zug, 12.Komp Pz.Gren.Rgt 2

1 Zug, 10.Komp Pz.Gren.Rgt 2

Followed by

Kampfgruppe Command elements

Commander of Kampfgruppe Obersturmbannführer Jochen Peiper

Commander Panzer Regiment 1 Sturmbannführer Werner Poetschke

Commander III Abt Pz.Gren.Rgt 2 Hauptsturmführer Jupp Diefenthal

Followed by

Main body of Kampfgruppe

1.Komp I Abt Pz.Rgt 1 (Panthers) Obersturmführer Karl Kremser

11.Komp III Abt Pz.Gren.Rgt. 2 Obersturmführer Heinz Tomhardt

6.Komp II Abt Pz.Rgt 1 (Mk IVs) Obersturmführer Benoni Junker

9.Komp Pz.Pi. Pz.Rgt 1 (-) Untersturmführer Erich Rumpf

7.Komp II Abt. Pz.Rgt 1 (Mk IVs) Hauptsturmführer Oskar Klingelhofer

10.Komp (Pz. Flak) Pz.Rgt 1 Obersturmführer Karl-Heinz Vogler

3.Komp Pz.Pi. Abteilung I Obersturmführer Franz Sievers

2.Komp I Abt Pz.Rgt 1 (Panthers) Obersturmführer Friedrich Christ

13.(sch) Komp III Abt. Pz.Gren.Rgt 2 (-) Untersturmführer Koch

12. (s) Komp III Abt. Pz.Gren.Rgt 2 (-) Untersturmführer Jochen Thiele

9.Komp III Abt. Pz.Gren. Rgt 2 Untersturmführer Max Leike

Followed by

501 (sch) Panzer Abteilung (King Tigers) Obersturmbannführer Hein von Westernhagen

84th Flak Abteilung Major von Sacken (Luftwaffe)

II Abt. Panzer Artillerie Rgt 1 Hauptsturmführer Kalischko

Echelons

Supply, repair and services columns

these was the Spitzen Kompanie commanded by Hauptsturmführer Georg Preuss, and formed from his 10 Company, Panzergrenadier Regiment 2 (Pz.Gren.Rgt.2), one platoon of pioneers from 9 Company, Pz.Rgt 1, and a platoon of heavy weapons from 12 Company, Pz.Gren.Rgt.2.

The main body of the kampfgruppe was formed by the remainder of Panzer Regiment 1 and Panzergrenadier Regiment 2. This was to follow between seven and ten minutes behind Preuss's advance guard. Bringing up the rear of the column was von Westernhagen's battalion, the Luftwaffe flak guns, and Kalischko's artillery pieces, following some fifteen minutes behind the main body. Peiper's command group would deploy between the *spitze* and Preuss's advance guard, or between Preuss and the main body, as the situation dictated.

Peiper calculated that the whole column would stretch for 25km along the single road on which it would travel. It would take two hours for the column to pass a given point. This was far from an ideal situation, but Peiper seems

to have been confident of his success as he awaited the opening of the barrage at 05:30 hrs on 16 December 1944.

Reviewing the attack force prior to *Wacht am Rhein.*

By dawn on the
morning of 17
December 1944 the
Germans had
advanced eight
miles west of their
start points.

Chapter Three

16 DECEMBER 1944:
PEIPER FRUSTRATED

At 05:35 hrs on the morning of 16 December the Ardennes front exploded as hundreds of guns and werfers (rocket launchers) opened up a massive bombardment, which marked the beginning of Hitler's great offensive. Twenty-year-old 1st Lieutenant Lyle Bouck and the eighteen men of his I & R (Intelligence and Reconnaissance) Platoon, 394th Infantry Regiment, 99th Division, were on the receiving end in their prepared positions in Lanzerath:

> *Some time before dawn, the artillery fire began. I don't know how long it lasted but it seemed like a long time. At first it went over our heads. Then they started to hit in front of Lanzerath. There was a short lull before quite a bit began to drop on our positions. I had the impression that we had been bracketed. It was intermittent for more than an hour, a lot of tree bursts.*

Tree bursts were lethal, as the wood splinters added to the shrapnel caused by the bursting shells. Bouck reports that he and his men were 'in a shocked and stunned state', and he began to wonder when the platoon would begin to sustain casualties. Fortunately his men were sheltering in prepared positions with a good covering of logs as overhead protection. Bouck reported the barrage back to regimental headquarters, but was informed that the regiment was taking heavy fire all along the line, and warned to be 'doubly alert'.

During the night of the 15/16 December thousands of German troops positioned themselves for the attack. Kampfgruppe Peiper moved into assembly areas in the Blankenheimer Wald, either side of Reichstrasse 51, to the north-east of Dahlem. Obersturmführer Flacke, adjutant of the SPW battalion (III.(gep.)/Pz.Gren.Regt. 2) described the battalion's move:

> *My commander, Hauptsturmführer Diefenthal, ordered me to assemble the battalion on the forest trail and lead it to the march route in the assigned march order through the Blankenheimer Wald.*
>
> *The lead panzer [SPW] was Obersturmführer Preuss's command panzer. He was commander of the 10th Company. I climbed into his panzer and directed the battalion in a night march to the deployment route behind Blankenheim.*
>
> *As prescribed in the regimental order, the individual units of our battalion organized themselves into the battle group's march formation.*

While Peiper and his men waited in their deployment areas, the infantry of the 12th Volksgrenadier Division attempted to break through the American lines, thus opening a gap for Peiper to lead his men through on their dash for

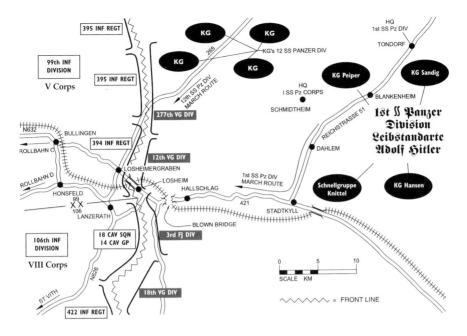

Map labels:

- 395 INF REGT
- 99th INF DIVISION
- V Corps
- 395 INF REGT
- KG
- KG
- KG
- KG
- KG's 12 SS PANZER DIV
- 265
- 12th SS Pz DIV MARCH ROUTE
- 277th VG DIV
- HQ I SS Pz CORPS
- SCHMIDTHEIM
- HQ 1st SS Pz DIV
- TONDORF
- KG Peiper
- KG Sandig
- BLANKENHEIM
- 1st SS Panzer Division Leibstandarte Adolf Hitler
- REICHSTRASSE 51
- DAHLEM
- N632
- BULLINGEN
- ROLLBAHN C
- 394 INF REGT
- 12th VG DIV
- LOSHEIMERGRABEN
- ROLLBAHN D
- LOSHEIM
- HALLSCHLAG
- 1st SS Pz DIV MARCH ROUTE
- Schnellgruppe Knittel
- KG Hansen
- HONSFELD
- 99 XX 106
- LANZERATH
- 421
- STADTKYLL
- 106th INF DIVISION
- VIII Corps
- 18 CAV SQN 14 CAV GP
- 3rd FJ DIV
- BLOWN BRIDGE
- ST VITH
- N626
- 18th VG DIV
- 422 INF REGT
- 0   5   10
- SCALE KM
- ⌇⌇⌇⌇ = FRONT LINE

I SS Panzer Corps deployment areas and detail of German frontline forces.

German troops try to extract a vehicle from the mud. This illustrates the state of many of the roads along which Kampfgruppe Peiper had to advance. *(Airborne Forces Museum)*

the Meuse. But Peiper would have to wait.

Generalmajor Gerhard Engels sent his 27th and 48th Volksgrenadier Regiments against the American 99th Division's 394th Regiment, which defended the line between Losheimergraben and Losheim. Peiper spent most of the day at Engels' headquarters near Hallschlag, monitoring the infantry's progress, and waiting for the opportunity to give the order for his kampfgruppe to advance. He must have been very disappointed, not to say frustrated, by 12 Volksgrenadier's (VG) lack of progress, for although they had managed to capture Losheim, they had not managed to break through the 394th's line.

At the southern end of the 394th's area of responsibility, Lyle Bouck and his men saw the advance develop. After a couple of hours the artillery barrage ceased, and much to Bouck's surprise none of his men had been hurt. Bouck could hear small arms fire to the north around Losheimergraben, and to his rear at Bucholz Station, although the area to his front remained quiet. At about 08:30 Bouck and his men heard motors start up, and much to their chagrin realized that the tank destroyers of the 14th Cavalry were withdrawing towards Bucholz Station, leaving the I & R Platoon very much alone. Bouck had only sixteen M1 rifles, two carbines and two .30-calibre machine guns with which to defend his position.

Shortly after the withdrawal of the tank destroyers, Bouck received orders from regiment to occupy a house below his position, which had previously been occupied by artillery observers. Bouck took three men with him and occupied the house. From the upper floor he could see the road approaching the village from the east where it came over a crest about 600 yards away. Through his field glasses he could see a column of troops coming into view – Germans, wearing the distinctive paratrooper helmet – members of the 9th Parachute Regiment. Bouck withdrew to his main position, leaving two men to observe the advancing Germans and report back to him. He also requested artillery support, but none was available.

The I & R Platoon then received a welcome reinforcement, Lieutenant Warren Springer and three enlisted men, a forward observation team from C Battery of the 371st Field Artillery Battalion. Springer immediately volunteered to join Bouck, and was calling in artillery fire on Lanzerath when his jeep was hit and its radio was knocked out.

The two men Bouck had left in Lanzerath attempted to fall back to the main position, as German paratroopers were approaching the building they were in. While this was happening Bouck reported the approach of another German column:

> While all this was going on, here comes a German column up the road, walking north towards us, single file on both sides of the road, their weapons slung. They were singing as they marched.

Bouck prepared to ambush the approaching German column, which seemed to be completely unaware of the American presence. Unfortunately, before the Germans came within close range they were warned by a girl from the village

German Fallschirmjager. A battalion of the 9th Fallschirmjager Regiment was attached to Kampfgruppe Peiper at Lanzerath, and elements of the unit continued serving with Peiper until the breakout from La Gleize.

and dispersed quickly, followed by a volley of shots from Bouck's men. After a long pause the Germans advanced again, as Bouck describes:

Then after maybe an hour and a half they came screaming and yelling, in a direct frontal assault up the snow covered hill. They were firing at us but they had no targets. And there was a typical farm fence that bisected the hill. The paratroopers had to climb over this fence. For us it was like target practice ....

Then they stopped coming. Someone waved a red flag and in poor English yelled, 'Medics! Medics!' It was approaching noon.

For about forty-five minutes the Germans tended their wounded and prepared to attack again. During the third attack Private Risto Milosevich found himself alone in a foxhole manning a machine gun. He described the German attack as 'like shooting clay ducks at the amusement park'. He was joined by the platoon sergeant, Bill Snape, who took over firing the machine gun while Milosevich fed the ammunition. They fired so many rounds at the approaching Germans, who got to within thirty yards or their position, that the barrel of the machine gun buckled and became inoperable.

Running short of ammunition after the third German attack, Bouck decided it was time to pull his men out:

It was late in the day, but still light, somewhere between three-thirty and four-thirty in the afternoon. I sent word that when I blew a whistle three times everyone would leave their foxholes with their weapons. We'd rendezvous at a point on the road. We would move by night through the woods. I told Snape and Tsak (Bill Tsakanikas) to remove the distributor caps from the jeeps.

Bouck and his men had little chance to escape, and he describes the final German attack during which he was wounded and captured:

Tsak was with me in a foxhole as we prepared to take off. I heard the sounds of boots and Germans hollering as they fired. I had one full magazine left in my carbine. I saw two Germans running towards us. I had filed the sere [the sere holds back the working parts of a weapon and thus prevents it from firing more than one shot each time the trigger is pulled] *off my carbine, so when I squeezed the trigger it operated like a machine gun. I emptied a clip at those two. I was satisfied I had fired my last round.*

I saw the muzzle of a gun poke into our hole. I pushed Tsakanikas to get him out of the way and then someone yelled, 'How many of you?' I didn't speak much German but I answered, 'Zwei! Zwei!' With that came a burst of gunfire.

Then the two were helped from the foxhole. Both were wounded, Bouck in the foot and Tsakanikas with serious facial injuries. As Bouck was being led back to Lanzerath, carrying Tsakanikas, another German soldier approached:

He kept asking if we had been at St-Lo. I answered 'Nein, nein.' He started screaming about his comrades at St-Lo. Shit, I didn't know what else to say. Then he stuck a gun in my back and pulled the trigger. I don't know whether it was a misfire or the gun was empty. But someone said, 'Raus. Raus.' He disappeared and we went into Lanzerath.

Bouck and Tsakanikas were taken into a room which served as both a first-aid station and the headquarters of the 9th Fallschirmjager Regiment.

While Bouck had been busy driving off the successive attacks at Lanzerath, Jochen Peiper was still waiting for the breakthrough to come. At around 16:00 he received orders to move his kampfgruppe forward to Losheim in readiness. The kampfgruppe's forward move was difficult and time-consuming as the roads towards the front were blocked by the infantry divisions' artillery and supply trains.

By 17:00 Peiper's lead elements had reached the Scheid railway bridge, only to find it had been blown. With no suitable bridging equipment near to hand, Peiper ordered his advance elements to detour down a dirt track to the right of the bridge and cross the railway line. At about this time Peiper received further orders to move through Hullschied and then on to Lanzerath, a change brought about by the 12th VG's inability to break through the American lines at Losheimergraben. It was during this detour that the kampfgruppe received its first casualties, as described by Obersturmführer Werner Sternebeck:

The Scheid road bridge over the railway, blown by the retreating Germans in September 1944. Peiper detoured down the track to the right and crossed the railway tracks.

Immediately west of Losheim the first Panzer V [Panther] drove into a minefield and was lost for the rest of the operation. After engineers removed the mines, the advance was cautiously continued. In the meantime, the sun had set. Uncertainty increased, we still saw nothing of the enemy.

There was another explosion and the second Panzer V drove into the next minefield, approximately 500 metres west of Losheim. Again the mines had to be found and removed. This took a lot of time. Our two Panthers, which were thought of as battering rams, were lost for the rest of the deployment without having made any contact with the enemy.

Immediately south-east of Merlscheid at an open road obstacle my panzer jumped and came to a stand-still after a detonation. Now it was also lost.

Sternebeck took over another tank, and the march continued. Peiper had lost three tanks from his advance guard, and his men had not yet made contact with the enemy!

All the delays conspired to postpone Kampfgruppe Peiper's arrival at Lanzerath until almost midnight. As soon as he arrived at Lanzerath Peiper had a heated discussion with Oberst Helmut von Hofmann, commander of 9th Fallschirmjager Regiment, which was observed by Lyle Bouck:

A cuckoo clock on the wall sounded off when it reached midnight. That meant December 17. That meant I had reached my twenty-first birthday ....

Just about this time I realized that a furious argument was going on. An SS officer was pounding his fist as he tried to show a map on a bureau. He gave that up and stabbed the map on the wall with two bayonets. While he was shouting at another officer, messengers came and went; the SS officer spoke to them. I could hear the sounds of tanks and other heavy vehicles. This went on well after midnight, until a few hours before dawn.

The other officer mentioned by Bouck was Oberst Hofmann. Although Peiper was outranked by Hofmann he demanded to know the cause of the delay, and Peiper reported Hofmann's reason:

His answer was that the woods were heavily fortified and that scattered fire from prepared pillboxes, plus mines in the road, were holding up the advance. He told me it was impossible to advance under these circumstances.

I asked him if he had personally reconnoitred the American positions in the woods, and he replied he had received information from one of his battalion commanders. I asked the battalion commander and he said he had got the information from a captain in his battalion. I called the captain and he answered that he had not personally seen the Americans. At this point I became very angry and ordered the paratroop regiment to give me one battalion and I would lead the breakthrough.

The attack was set for 04:00. Two Panthers would lead the column, followed by a series of armoured half-tracks and then a mixture of Panther and Mk IV tanks. Strangely enough, we broke through the area without firing a shot and found it completely unoccupied.

Peiper had had a very frustrating day. Instead of being well on his way to the Meuse he had yet to penetrate the American lines. Small groups of American soldiers, such as Lyle Bouck's I & R Platoon, had caused delays in many places, and these would have a major effect on the success of the offensive.

The building on the left was originally the Café Scholzen. It was the headquarters of the 9th Fallschirmjager Regiment. It was in this building that Lyle Bouck witnessed the discussion between Peiper and Hoffman at around midnight on 16 December 1944.

Chapter Four

17 DECEMBER 1944:
BREAKTHROUGH

At 04:00 on 17 December the kampfgruppe began its advance through the American lines. It would take the 800 vehicles all day to pass through Lanzerath, and the lead elements would reach Stavelot by the time the tail of the column had transited the town.

Hauptsturmführer Preuss's 10 Company, Pz.Gren.Rgt 2, took over the lead from Sternebeck's armoured *spitze*. Their SPWs were faster and better suited to leading an attack through close terrain. The *spitze* followed 10 Company, with a company of paratroopers riding on the panzers, and the three remaining companies of paratroopers escorting the advance on foot. It was quickly seen that these preparations were not required, as neither a minefield nor American positions existed. Hofmann had received his information from a battalion commander, who had received it from a company commander, who had, in turn, received it from a platoon leader, and the non-existent American troops may simply have been an excuse not to advance into a heavily forested area after dark, particularly after a hard day's fighting. It is understandable that Peiper was very angry, having lost another six precious hours.

Once the woods had been passed Obersturmführer Werner Sternebeck's *spitze* once more assumed the lead:

> On leaving the woods north of Lanzerath, we made our first contact with the enemy, who apparently, quickly withdrew without being drawn into combat.

The kampfgruppe's advance from 04:00 to 23:00, 17 December 1944.

The Losheimergraben railroad station [Bucholz Station], immediately to the right of our route to Honsfeld was occupied by the enemy. These enemy forces did not stop us. Nevertheless the advance slowed in the uncertainty of darkness.

One of the American soldiers in the path of the kampfgruppe was Lance Corporal Dick Byers, who with Sergeant Curtis Fletcher and Lieutenant Harold Meyer formed a forward observation team from the 371st Field Artillery. On the night of the 16th they had arrived at a farmhouse close to Bucholz Station. The farmhouse was occupied by a few men from K Company, 394th Infantry Regiment (IR), and had a first-aid station in its cellar. After a stint on guard duty Byers went to sleep, to be woken by a GI telling him that there were tanks outside. Byers rolled over and went back to sleep. Several minutes later Lieutenant Meyer spotted Byers and Fletcher still asleep, and woke them. As the pair got dressed a decision was taken to head for the barn, where their jeep was parked, and use its radio to call artillery down on the German tanks as they negotiated a sharp bend in the road. Byers takes up the story:

As we opened the back door of the barn, we saw three German paratroopers silhouetted against the white snow, but they couldn't see us with the black

Members of the kampfgruppe pass through a Belgian village during their advance. Note the abandoned American equipment, including an M3 half-track. *(Airborne Forces Museum)*

courtyard behind us. Since they appeared armed with Schmeissers [sub-machine guns] *and had the backing of an entire panzer battle group, we decided not to argue over possession of the radio. We took off through a side gate into a patch of pinewoods parallel to the road.*

Once they were in the woods the three headed north. Unfortunately, at some point during the journey Fletcher became separated from the other two, and was subsequently captured. Byers and Meyer continued north, bypassing Honsfeld from where the sound of gunfire could be heard. At Hunningen they reached the relative safety of 2nd Division's lines. After relating their experiences, Byers and Meyer were told that the 2nd Division men were 'old-timers sent down to save our inexperienced asses'!

Having bypassed Bucholz Station, Sternebeck's *spitze* continued towards Honsfeld, where he reports:

At approx 04:30 hrs, we reached Honsfeld. In town standing on the right side of the road in our direction of march, was an armoured column (tanks, armoured personnel carriers, jeeps) – a reconnaissance unit [part of 14th Cavalry]. *Since I thought it was a unit from 'Einsatzgruppe Greif' I stopped next to the column to make contact. I dismounted from my panzer and climbed onto the other and looked for the 'Z' designation on the turret. Unfortunately, my search was in vain. I was standing next to the enemy, who dozed. My reaction was to climb back into my panzer, beat a quick retreat to the north-western exit from the town and report the presence of the enemy to the panzer battalion.*

Einsatzgruppe Greif was part of Otto Skorzeny's decoy operation, and were partly equipped with American equipment. Realizing his mistake, Sternebeck remounted his own panzer and departed rapidly towards Bullingen. He would leave the capture of Honsfeld to the kampfgruppe's main body.

At about 06:00 the main body of the kampfgruppe arrived at Honsfeld, to find the Americans still sleeping, as is reported by Jochen Peiper:

At first light, when we entered Honsfeld at high speed, we woke an American reconnaissance battalion. The anti-tank guns at the entrance to the town were unmanned. The streets, alleys and yards were filled with armoured vehicles, jeeps and trucks, and the sleepy eyes from hundreds of speechless GIs looked out of the windows. We drove on, firing a few bursts of machine-gun fire into the buildings, and continued in the direction of Bullingen. The Fallschirmjagers [paratroopers] *were supposed to clear out the town. The one company that occupied the lead panzer element remained with the battle group until the end of the offensive.*

One of the sleepy-eyed Americans was Private Jim Foley from the 394th IR. Honsfeld was one of the 99th Division's rest and recuperation centres, and Foley was enjoying a break from the front line. Foley and his comrades were still asleep when Peiper's vehicles entered the town:

We stayed in the sack until after 5:00 A.M., when we heard some heavy vehicles in the street. I decided to take a look, but before I had chance I heard a shot

Dead US soldiers in Honsfeld. Kampfgruppe Peiper passed through the town during the morning of 17 December 1944.

outside. Wooten from G Company ran into the room. All he had on were his long johns and he looked as funny as hell. He said, 'One of those silly damn guards of ours took a shot at me when I stepped out to take a piss.'

It sounded funny at the time but what we didn't know was that the 'guard' was a Jerry. I piled back in the sack until 6:30 A.M., when I heard Kraut voices in the street. I stuck my head outside to see a few of our recon cars burning across the street and three Kraut tanks very much intact! Then some bastard opened up on me with a burp gun and I got my ass back inside quick.

After an abortive attempt to escape through the back window of the house, Foley's group surrendered and were lined up in the street. Foley was lucky. Not all the prisoners captured at Honsfeld survived the experience, and this was to become a recurring theme during the kampfgruppe's advance. Siegfried Jaekel, a pioneer with the 3rd Panzer Pioneer Company, recounted seeing groups of American prisoners being executed, in a sworn statement at the post-war trial of many members of the kampfgruppe:

The first prisoners of war I recall seeing during the offensive were in the outskirts of Honsfeld, as we were leaving this town towards Bullingen. This was between 8 and 9 a.m., 17 December 1944. Just before turning right to go in the direction of Bullingen I remember passing an American truck which had a machine gun mounted above the cab. As we approached the intersection, I heard machine pistol fire coming from the right and later saw 15 Americans dead alongside the road.

Jaekel also stated that he had seen these men with their hands above their heads. Jaekel mentions another incident, one in which he participated, on the road to Bullingen, just after the column had been attacked by American aircraft:

Our group leader, Sepp Witkowski, ordered us to bump them off [Eight American prisoners]! Witkowski fired at them with his machine pistol and Hergeth with his rifle. They were unarmed and held their hands in surrender position. I shot at them with my pistol for two or three rounds.

Jaekel goes on to report several other cases in Bullingen and on the Thirimont road, but his most damning statement is that he 'saw and heard of so many American prisoners of war who had been shot or were being shot during this offensive that I cannot remember every case'! It should be borne in mind that Jaekel was on trial and had turned 'state's evidence' to try and save his own life. That said, there were a number of instances of American prisoners and civilians being shot by the kampfgruppe, and this will be looked at in more detail shortly.

At about the same time as Jochen Peiper entered Honsfeld, his *spitze* commander Werner Sternebeck encountered an American convoy:

At 06:00 hrs the lead panzer element surprised a truck column coming from the direction of Bullingen, north of Honsfeld. The column was brought to a halt by blinking a red flashlight. It was a supply column of about eight trucks. It was overpowered without firing a shot.

Sternebeck goes on to recount his unit's next engagement with the enemy, just south of Bullingen:

Continuing on toward Bullingen, approx 07:00 hrs, we received fire from automatic weapons approx 1,500 to 2,000m south of the edge of the town and west of the march route. The lead panzer elements veered off, returned fire and attacked an airfield containing reconnaissance aircraft. Peiper 'whistled' us on and urged us to hasten the advance to capture Bullingen.

Peiper was continually driving his lead elements on, leaving the clearing of American defensive positions to his main body. He had a very good reason for pushing Sternebeck to capture Bullingen – a fuel dump. The chances of fuel convoys reaching Peiper before he reached his objective, the Meuse crossings, were very slim, and he had been ordered to make use of captured American supplies to refuel his vehicles. One such supply dump was in Bullingen.

The American troops manning the roadblocks to the south of Bullingen were the 254th ECB, part of the 1121st Engineer Group, and had been operating under the command of the 99th Division. A, B and C Companies of the 254th were to dig in on the southern approaches to the town, where they would find tank destroyers and light tanks already manning the roadblocks. As the Engineer companies arrived at their assigned positions there was no sign of this armoured support. B Company was dug in astride the Honsfeld road, and was the first to contact Peiper's *spitze*:

At approximately 5:00 a.m. flares appeared on our Company B front as tracked vehicles were coming in our direction. The first positive identification was shouts that were heard in German. The first order was given by Lieutenant Huff, Company B, who opened fire with rifles, rifle grenades, and machine guns.

The time of contact differs from that reported by Sternebeck, although B Company's weaponry fits in with his report of receiving 'automatic weapons' fire. In a confused fight the Engineers were driven back through Bullingen, losing many casualties in the process, particularly from B Company. The Engineer after-action report states that the Germans attacked three times before they overran B Company's position, and suffered heavy losses. Sternebeck considered it a minor incident, but did admit to losing a Mk IV.

With Sternebeck's advance guard ordered to move on, Hauptsturmführer Preuss's 10 Company continued with the elimination of the airfield. Untersturmführer Asschendorff's heavy platoon destroyed six spotter planes. As Preuss's men pushed into Bullingen they were fired on from the houses on both sides of the street, possibly by members of the 254th ECB who were withdrawing through the town. Preuss suffered a number of losses, as he reported:

Untersturmführer Asschendorff had strict orders from me to take care that all of my company's SPWs stayed closed up. This was his most important mission at the end of the company. I suffered losses in Bullingen, including my two platoon leaders (Oberscharführer Otto and Hauptscharführer Knobloch. Both from head wounds). The Amis fired down out of the houses into our open SPWs and I had to get out of the city as quickly as possible. As I myself took the lead, there was no one else behind me. Wedged into a fleeing American column, I was carried into the enemy rear areas. Escaping into the open country was impossible, since my five men with three rifles and two pistols – I must have shoved my machine gun into the hands of Untersturmführer Bahrend back in Losheim – could not have defended ourselves against the large group of men around us. Only in a big patch of woods was I successful in breaking free, but even here I twice had to change positions as brief fire-fights developed with retreating American infantry groups. Then, however, we fought our way back to the troops.

Preuss was not the only member of the kampfgruppe to go astray in Bullingen. As Sternebeck led his *spitze* through Bullingen he took a wrong turn:

Back on the road to Bullingen, at a blind spot several hundred metres from the entrance to the town, the Panzer IV in front of me was destroyed by close-combat weapons [probably a bazooka, as reported by the 254th ECB]. *The crew was shot while dismounting. No one survived! Driving wildly and firing*

Members of the Leibstandarte during the advance on 17 December 1944. Behind the two officers is an SdKfz 251 SPW. *(Airborne Forces Museum)*

from all weapons, the rest of the lead panzer element entered Bullingen. The enemy was in total confusion. We had achieved surprise. There was no organized enemy resistance apparent. The confusion also affected us. We became completely muddled in the town and drove to the north in the direction of Wirtzfeld instead of to the west. After driving approx 1,200 to 1,500m north of Bullingen we began to take anti-tank fire from the north-west. Another Panzer IV from the lead panzer element was hit. The panzer was hit in the turret, the commander mortally wounded. We could not make out the enemy, but we re-established radio contact and were summoned back. We drove fast through Bullingen to the western exit. The lead panzer element now consisted of only two Panzer IVs and an engineer squad. We drove along the Bullingen-Butgenbach road to 'Domane' where an American first-aid station was established. Although the surgeons approached us in order to surrender the first-aid station, we turned to the south along the Bullingen-Moderscheid road.

Once it had refuelled, the kampfgruppe continued its march towards Ligneuville. Along the way Sternebeck rejoined the column and assumed his assigned place at the lead. The kampfgruppe continued to Thirimont via Schoppen and Ondenvaal. While Preuss's company was able to continue along the dirt tracks, taking the direct route to the main Malmedy–Vielsalm road, the remainder of the kampfgruppe had to detour along the Waimes road until it too reached the Malmedy–Vielsalm road at the Baugnez crossroads.

On collision course with Kampfgruppe Peiper was B Battery, 285th Field Artillery Observation Battalion, about 140 men all told. Lieutenant Colonel Dave Pergrin, commanding 291st ECB, had been ordered to defend Malmedy with part of his unit, by Colonel Wallace Anderson, commanding 1111th Engineer Group. Reports had reached Pergrin that a German armoured column had passed through Bullingen, and he expected an attack at any time. In actual fact the German column was Kampfgruppe Peiper, and had no intention of attacking Malmedy. Pergrin tried to gather any troops he could to help in the defence of the town. Towards noon possible reinforcements arrived, as Pergrin reported:

At 11:35 a.m. things began to happen. Major Boyer, battalion commander of the 7th Armoured Division's Tank Destroyers, came into town. We halted him in front of the CP [command post] and asked him to form on our defences. He gave us a negative reply when he advised us that his mission was to move to the defence of the 106th Division at St. Vith. Following closely behind Major Boyer came Battery B of the 285th Field Artillery Observation Battalion, the guys who give target designation for our artillery. They were led by two officers and a driver in a jeep. Although this group had nothing but rifles to aid our cause, it could add at least 100 men to the defence.

In the jeep were a Captain Mills and a Lieutenant Virgil Lary. They would not remain in Malmedy as I requested since their mission was also in St Vith.

Mills and Lary were warned about the proximity of the German armoured column and advised to detour towards Stavelot, rather than continuing down the Ligneuville road. They chose to ignore this advice, and Dave Pergrin continues the story:

Mills and Lary followed Boyer out of the town on the way to Baugnez, just beyond Sergeant Charles Dishaw's Company B roadblock, where they were to turn south towards Ligneuville and thence on to St Vith. They never got to St Vith!

Sometime in the early afternoon we heard the firing of heavy weapons and what sounded like machine pistols, then there was a pause. A while later more sounds of bigger guns and again what sounded like machine guns and pistols. Just prior to this, one of Captain Conlin's patrols had reported in with the sighting of German tanks in great numbers on the way out of Thirimont.

We now knew that Battery B of the 285th was in trouble and the breakaway kampfgruppe was at our doorstep. Just before this I had been concerned about their progress towards St Vith. There was nothing that we could do now but attempt to determine if they had met up with the Germans. I took Sergeant Crickenberger and a jeep out to Dishaw's roadblock and learned from him that the firing had ceased. However, it had not been far away. We continued out to Geromont, parked the jeep, and walked through a pasture towards a line of trees.

Half running, babbling incoherently, dishevelled and without helmets, came three men. We soon realized that they were Americans who turned out to be men of the 285th. We put them in the jeep and brought them to our aid station in Malmedy where I learned that they were Sergeant Kenneth Ahrens, Mike Shiranko, and Albert Valenzi. Once their wounds were treated and they had coffee, they told a clear story of an out-and-out massacre.

Baugnez crossroads – the 'Malmedy Massacre'.

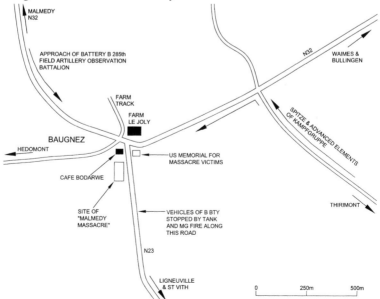

So this was how the Americans, and the world at large, came to hear of what has come to be called the Malmedy massacre, although the events actually took place several miles to the south at the crossroads hamlet of Baugnez. What had happened to B Battery?

As the American battery headed south from Malmedy, Werner Sternebeck's *spitze* was approaching the crossroads. Sternebeck writes:

> *During an observation halt on the road from Thirimont to the north-west, about 800 to 1,200m east of the Baugnez intersection, I saw an enemy truck column negotiating the intersection moving south. The lead panzer element opened fire (high-explosive shells) against the travelling column, which was located about 200 to 300m south of the intersection. Several vehicles immediately caught fire, the column became confused and the vehicles began running off the road and into each other. The crews dismounted and sought cover. That was the moment to attack across the Waimes-Baugnez road to the intersection. Before reaching the intersection we were hit by machine-gun fire and rifle fire from the dismounted crews. We returned fire with our on-board machine guns and hastened our attack into the standing column. When my lead panzer had approached to within 60-70m of the column the Americans stood up from the roadside ditch and raised their hands in surrender.*

Sternebeck ordered the surrendering Americans to move back towards the crossroads, before continuing on to Ligneuville, often referred to as Engelsdorf in German accounts. Jochen Peiper was travelling close behind his lead element in a captured American jeep. He reports:

> *I suddenly heard my cannons and machine guns open fire. I realized that the point had hit the main road from Malmedy to Petit Thier and I drove off to the*

View from the Thirimont road of the N62 from Malmedy to St Vith. It was from close to this spot that Sternebeck's *spitze* opened fire on B Battery near Baugnez crossroads.

Baugnez crossroads. The American prisoners were assembled in the field on the right-hand side of the road. It was in this field that the massacre took place.

point in the jeep. The column behind me was detached, since the piece of road was exceptionally difficult.

About five tanks and the same number of half-tracks were standing in front of me and they were shooting with all weapons at their disposal. I saw that it was an American truck convoy. I gave an order to cease fire several times, since I was annoyed at having my armoured spearhead held up, in view of the fact they had lost so much time already. Furthermore, I was annoyed at having these beautiful trucks, which we needed so badly, all shot up.

In another account of the events at Baugnez, Peiper writes:

When we reached the road intersection and turned south the pass was partially blocked by a crashed and burning truck. We found a number of US soldiers, estimated at 60, in the roadside ditch and in a field. Besides those who had been killed or wounded by our fire, the men could practically be divided into three groups. One group came towards us with their hands held behind their helmets in surrender. We directed them to the rear because the mission of the following

N62 towards Ligneuville. Peiper ordered Sternebeck to press on down this road to Ligneuville after passing through Baugnez.

infantry was to assemble prisoners we captured along our route of advance. Group two lay next to the road and played dead. I specifically remember several of our soldiers firing warning shots. The third group also played dead, but they were closer to the nearby forest. These soldiers tried to make their way, unobserved, to the edge of the forest and we fired several shots at them. The lead element then drove off in the direction of Engelsdorf [Ligneuville], while the prisoners of war, on their own more or less, unsupervised, assembled at the road intersection.

Peiper is also reported to have shouted 'It's a long way to Tipperary, boys!' at the American prisoners as he drove past them. Sternebeck's *spitze* had disappeared in the direction of Ligneuville, and Peiper found himself at the front of the column:

We had information there was an American command post in Ligneuville. Since I knew with certainty we would meet resistance in Ligneuville, I had no desire to be the first one to enter the town. I motioned to my rear and three half-tracks and the tank of 1st Leutnant Arndt Fischer, the adjutant of the 1st

Battalion, passed me by. They continued towards Ligneuville at great speed and I attached myself to their heels.

Peiper stated quite categorically that he did not see any prisoners shot, and went on to say:

There is more than one version of what later happened at the road intersection, but no one knows for sure, nor do I.

Supply Sergeant Bill Merriken's truck was the third vehicle in the convoy. A shell exploded just in front of it, and then several trucks behind him were hit. At this point Merriken and the remainder of the vehicle crews abandoned the trucks and took cover in a ditch. Merriken goes on to report:

The firing lasted maybe five or ten minutes. There was debris flying around and none of the guys could move out. Our view was obstructed because of trees and a bend in the road, but then a tank came, with its machine gun firing at the ditches. Lieutenant Lary said 'Surrender, boys.' The German in the tank said, 'Up, up, up,' and motioned us to go to the rear. As I went up the road, the tank fired. Then more vehicles passed and we were again motioned to hurry.

Another member of B Battery, Jim Mattera, was in one of the last trucks in the convoy. As his truck passed the crossroads all hell let loose:

We hit the crossroads, heading south. All at once 88s on tanks came down and they hit three vehicles behind me. Everybody jumped off, got down beside the road.

It is interesting that Mattera talks of 88mm guns on the tanks. This is a regular occurrence in Allied accounts – every gun an 88, and every tank a Tiger. The tanks engaging the convoy were Mk IVs and Panthers, both equipped with 75mm guns. Peiper's Tiger battalion had to use a road further south and would not rejoin the kampfgruppe until late on the 17th, as it reorganized on the hill above Stavelot. Mattera continues:

The panzers turned to their left at the crossroads. German soldiers suddenly come out through the woods with their automatics. It looks like a thousand of them. They were SS troops in black. I was in a ditch and it was a high-crowned road. One tank came down the road with a guy up on the machine gun. I'm laying there with my carbine and two fellows next to me. I had the carbine right on the guy's eyes and was ready to pull the trigger when they stopped me. 'You miss him, you son of a bitch, and our ass is mud.' I dropped my carbine. This SS trooper on the machine gun swung around and he directed us to walk to the crossroads. He spoke English.

While Peiper and his *spitze* carried on towards Ligneuville, American prisoners began to gather in a field south of the crossroads, to the west of the road. Vehicles of the kampfgruppe continued to pass down the road – as many as 600 vehicles passed through the Baugnez crossroads during the kampfgruppe's passage.

By approximately 14:00 hrs, 113 American prisoners had gathered in the field. About fifteen minutes later members of the kampfgruppe opened fire on the Americans – the reason for this is difficult to discern. Sixty-seven of the

Americans were killed, either in the first volleys of fire, or when German soldiers moved through the field shooting anyone who showed any sign of life. Forty-six GIs survived the shooting, many of them wounded, and four died later of the wounds they had received. The whole incident lasted about fifteen minutes. The men that Dave Pergrin had met at Geromont were some of the survivors.

There are two main schools of thought on why the SS men opened fire. The first sees their action as an out-and-out massacre of prisoners, while the second sees it as a response to American prisoners attempting to escape. Jim Mattera was close to the front of the gathered American prisoners when the shooting began:

Then we were ordered down to the field, I'm right in the front row, like cattle. My recollection I seen them setting up three tripods facing the field. There was an officer shouting to hurry up. Then I hear an officer command, 'Machen alle kaputt!' Kill them all. The machine gun bullets began. We all hit the ground, ten to fifteen minutes. I heard my buddies hollering. Haines, my buddy next to me on the ground, said, 'I'm hit, can you help me?' I said 'Lay still'. Then I

Smiling members of the Leibstandarte after the breakthrough on 17 December 1944.
(Airborne Forces Museum

heard him gurgle and die.

Bill Merriken had a different memory of the incident. After seeing a tank or SPW manoeuvring to try and bring its main gun to bear:

I figured they were going to blow us up. But they couldn't depress the gun enough. There was a lot of shouting and I saw a man with a pistol.

The 'man with a pistol' was later identified as Georg Fleps, a Romania-born SS volunteer. He stated that he obeyed an order from his commander, Oberscharführer Hans Siptrott, to open fire, a charge that Siptrott denied categorically:

I went across the field towards the crossroads and came to a stop some 300 metres below it. My other tanks, still moving on the road, also arrived at the crossroads. When I decided to get moving again, my loader Fleps, for reasons unknown to me, fired two shots with his pistol at the Americans, who in the meantime had been disarmed by the infantry. I kicked my loader in the back and hurt my shin. I was standing in my turret hatch and my intercom was switched on so that the crew could have heard me. My radio operator, Arnold, also had his radio turned on, and could later testify that Fleps had gotten no orders from me. It would also have been senseless to fire on someone with a pistol from 300 metres. I then headed towards Engelsdorf with my tanks. When I arrived with my unit, I reported the incident to my commander.

Siegfried Jaekel, who had already been involved in shooting at prisoners in Bullingen and Honsfeld, also admitted to having been a participant at Baugnez. His evidence is worth quoting at length:

Between 1:00 and 2:00 p.m. we arrived at a crossroads. This was three to five kilometres north of Ligneuville. I remember that there was a house and a barn on the right hand side of the road. South of the two buildings there was a hedgerow and a pasture. Parked on the right-hand side of the road was a panther tank with its cannon pointed at one o'clock. Just before we reached this tank, I saw approximately 60 to 80 American prisoners of war standing in a pasture.

In an SPW on the left hand side of the road were men of our unit with pistols in hand. There were also two other SPWs on the right hand side of the road. When we stopped here the Americans were standing in the pasture with their hands clasped above and behind their heads in a sign of surrender. They were unarmed and were not making any attempt to escape.

Before we came to a halt, I saw some SS officers present and some German soldiers in Panzer uniforms on a tank. As we passed Beutner's SPW we were given a signal to halt, and after we halted he spoke to Witkowski and told him the American prisoners were going to be shot. The men in my SPW loaded their weapons and made ready to fire into the prisoners. This took about three to five minutes before the first shots were fired.

At this time Hans Toedter and I were trying to get our machine gun ready; Pioneer Hans Stickel and Pioneer Harry Ende were doing the same thing with the rear machine gun. Jochim Hofman and Gustav Neve left our vehicle and stood at the rear of the SPW, Hofman aiming his machine pistol and Neve his fast-firing rifle at the prisoners who were standing in the field. I was serving as loader on the machine gun.

Witkowski left the SPW and stood on the road at the right front corner of our SPW aiming his machine pistol. Pioneer Hubert Storch stood with his rifle on the back of the SPW. Pioneer Hargeth stood near Storch with a rifle.

Pioneers Walkowiak and Scholtze, both of whom had rifles, stayed in the SPW. As we were making these preparations, I noticed the men in Losenski's SPW ahead of us were doing the same thing. At their front machine gun was Losenski. His assistant was Aistleitner and on their machine gun was Jirrasek, assisted by Wasenberger. The other men went to the ground with their rifles.

In Bode's SPW Kies was at the front machine gun assisted by Mueller. On the rear machine gun was a paratrooper and Horst Hummel. I remember that Bode posted himself in front of his SPW with his driver. Both of them were armed with machine pistols.

Then came Beutner's order to fire! The first shot was fired from Beutner's SPW. All of these men were firing from their positions into the Americans in the pasture. We fired about 75 rounds from the front machine guns. Then I went to the rear machine gun, loaded it and started shooting into the prisoners.

As soon as the firing started, all of the American prisoners who were in the field fell to the ground. While I was still in my SPW manning my machine gun, I saw the following additional people shooting into the American prisoners: Neve, Witkowski, Walkowiak, Scholtze, Storch, and Hergeth.

Then Sprenger's SPW pulled up behind ours and the men in the new arrival began firing into the prisoners. After the firing stopped our SPW was driven further down the road towards Engelsdorf. We stopped beside an American truck. Sprenger's SPW pulled up behind ours. I dismounted from the truck and began walking back towards the pasture. I was walking along the ditch when I saw Gettinger firing in the pasture from his SPW with his machine pistol.

Merriken, Mattera and Jaekel's accounts all give the strong impression that the shooting of the prisoners was premeditated. As has been previously mentioned, it should be borne in mind that Jaekel was giving evidence for his life, and was trying to implicate others to save his own neck.

So far the evidence points to a massacre of defenceless prisoners, but one piece of evidence, another signed statement by an American survivor, puts this in some doubt. One of the survivors, in a sworn statement countersigned by Lieutenant Raphael Schumacker, one of the chief prosecuting officers, wrote:

I decided to try to get away and walked slowly northwardly, but upon reaching a little dirt road or lane decided not to cross the lane or go around it. Sergeant Stabulis, Flack and I were together on this proposition. We turned around, slowly retraced our steps..... The group of soldiers in front of me were standing still and I slowly walked southwardly towards the fence at the south end of the field, more or less using the men in front as concealment. I know that Sergeant Stabulis and Pfc Flack were behind me. About two-thirds of the way towards the fence there were no more men to provide concealment so when I reached this point I ran towards the fence as hard as I could, crawled through it and then turned to my right and headed for the woods west of the field as fast as I could. Machine-gun fire was opened up at me but I was lucky enough to make it to the woods without getting hit and was picked up by the 30th Division a couple of days later.... I would like to add that as I came out from behind the crowd into the clear and headed for the south fence, two single shots were fired, which were either pistol or rifle in my opinion.

It is possible that a couple of warning shots were fired at the escapers, which then caused a general movement away from the road by the nervous American prisoners. This is supported by survivors who stated that they heard an American officer order them to 'Stand fast'. This general movement and the continued escape attempt could have caused the SS men to open fire. Shooting at prisoners attempting to escape is an acceptable act, but what followed is not. Siegfried Jaekel continues his account:

When we reached the pasture we entered it and stood for a few minutes to observe the Americans who were still moving, the three of us chose different targets and went towards them in order to shoot them. I went to a spot where I shot four or five wounded American prisoners with my pistol. I fired one shot into the heart of each wounded man. At the time I fired my pistol was one metre from the American soldiers at whom I fired. All of those men were moving or showing some sign of life before I fired. After I shot them they didn't move anymore. I am sure I killed every man at whom I fired.

Nine German soldiers entered the field and executed any wounded prisoners they found. Bill Merriken was lying wounded in the field:

The fellow next to me was delirious, moaning about being shot. I whispered to him to be still. He didn't stop. I heard footsteps of someone coming. He came to the fellow moaning and fired a pistol. The bullet went through my right knee. Part of the other man was on top of me and I figure he was shooting at him.

Jim Mattera was also lying in the field and remembered:

I heard tanks and half-tracks winding up, rrmmmm, rrmmmm. Down the road they come. Everyone who went by opened up with a machine gun. I heard one guy yell, 'You will cross the Siegfried line, you American bastards!' Brrrp! Jesus Christ, I thought they'd never stop. Finally, no more hollering. I'm laying there, about ten degrees that afternoon. Jesus Christ, my heart is in my mouth. I couldn't feel nothing burning. I kinda surmised when you're shot you're gonna hurt. When I hit the ground, my helmet flew off. I was twenty and had plenty of hair. I'm laying there bareheaded. Finally, I thought I heard somebody walking, there was maybe an inch or two of snow.

Somebody's here, I thought. Thank God I didn't open my eyes to look. I was too scared to open them. I heard this mild voice say, 'Hey Joe, you hurt? I'm here to help you, Joe.' Nobody answered. Then it was, 'Hey John, you hurt?' Guy said, 'Yeah, I'm hurt, I need help.' Boom! Oh, I thought, you dirty sons of bitches. I don't know how many of them there were, maybe two or three Germans, sent them in there, while they left one machine gun on the road.

Both Merriken and Mattera survived to tell their story.

Whether the initial shooting was caused by a premeditated decision to execute the prisoners or a reaction to attempted escapes, the subsequent execution of the wounded, at point blank range, is inexcusable. Michael Reynolds, in his book *The Devil's Adjutant* sums up the 'massacre':

They found themselves in a frenzy of killing. But this is neither in accordance with the normally accepted 'rules of war' nor with the Geneva Convention. Such actions are unacceptable and must be condemned by any civilized society. Having said that, which 20th century army has a blameless record?

While these events were taking place at the Baugnez crossroads, Jochen Peiper and his advance guard were driving hard for Ligneuville. Peiper had been informed by a prisoner that an American headquarters, the 49th AAA Brigade and its commander, Brigadier General Timberlake, were located in the village. Werner Sternebeck was at the front of the column with his *spitze*:

We entered Engelsdorf and advanced to the bridge over the Ambleve. On orders from panzer group, the lead panzer element was to stop the advance and secure the bridge. Engineers searched the bridge for explosives and were wounded by enemy machine-gun fire for their efforts.

When medics, designated by red crosses on their chests, backs and helmets, moved to fetch the wounded, the enemy machine guns grew silent. This was repeated several times. Then the machine guns could be wiped out. Opposite the church was a large hotel. The hotelkeeper appeared to be waiting for us. I ordered a halt in order to question him about enemy soldiers. I was so surprised by his reply that I can still tell you what he said today: 'Good day, Herr Offizier, the Herr General has left with his staff a few minutes ago, but will return by Christmas.' Surprised by this information, I left my panzer, walked into the hotel and discovered that the lunch table had still not been cleared. Burning cigarettes and unfinished drinks confirmed the sudden flight of the brigade staff.

Ligneuville from the Ambleve bridge. The Hotel du Moulin, on the left of the church, was Brigadier General Timberlake's headquarters.

Timberlake and his staff had had a very close call, departing only minutes before the Germans arrived. Not all the Americans in Ligneuville left without a fight. Several minutes behind Sternebeck came the command group. Untersturmführer Arndt Fischer, Adjutant, Pz.Rgt.1, was in the lead Panther of the group:

> *Sternebeck was ahead of us by a few minutes with two Pz IVs and two SPWs in Engelsdorf. Behind me came the SPW with Peiper and Diefenthal. At first I drove carefully into the village, noticed no fighting, and tried to speed across the bridge. On the curve in front of the bridge I was knocked out from behind. A tank hidden by a house had let me run right into a trap. Sternebeck had still had the advantage of surprise. They were waiting for me.*

The tank referred to was a broken-down Sherman dozer, in the process of being repaired. As Fischer says, the Americans had been taken by surprise by Sternebeck's arrival, and had no chance to engage him. Fischer was a different story, and his tank was struck in the rear and set on fire:

> *As we abandoned our vehicle, we were fired on by rifles and machine guns from the surrounding houses. We burned like torches because we had fuelled up our tanks from drums and jerrycans a few hours previously in Bullingen, and we had also thoroughly soaked our clothes in the process. Peiper, who had wanted to give me covering fire from his SPW while taking the bridge, was able, I believe, to keep the riflemen in the houses off our backs. Except for our outstanding driver, our comrade Wolfgang Simon, the entire crew was able to get out of the vehicle.*

Peiper was following close behind Fischer:

> *Just before entering the town, I suddenly saw in front of me the tank of Lieutenant Fischer. It had been set on fire. I stopped about 50 yards from that vehicle and recognized a Sherman about 80 metres to my right. He was just about to aim his cannon at my vehicle. I ordered the driver to pull back at once and we remained at a protected corner of a house. Another half-track which followed us passed us by and was knocked out at that moment. I, myself, took a rocket-launcher and ran into a house in order to knock out the Sherman from the rear window but it was knocked out at that very moment by another tank.*

Peiper may be in error as to what knocked out the American dozer tank, as some evidence points to the tank being engaged and destroyed by a 251/9 SPW, which mounted a short 75mm gun. Two other Sherman tanks and a tank destroyer, in the town to be refitted, were also captured and destroyed. Peiper personally dressed Fischer's wounds. Fischer, who could not be evacuated until the next day, spent the night in Timberlake's bed in the Hotel du Moulin, 'under the Stars and Stripes'.

Once the town had been cleared, the kampfgruppe pushed on towards Stavelot and its crucial bridge over the Amblève. If the river could be crossed at Stavelot the kampfgruppe could push on to Trois Ponts and then to Werbomont. Passing through Pont Beaumont and Lodomez, Peiper's advance guard arrived on the hill to the south-east of Stavelot after dark.

Moving slowly along the narrow Rue du Vieux Chateau, with a steep hill to its left, and a precipitous drop into the river valley to its right, the lead tank was crawling around a sharp corner, when a shout of 'Halt!' challenged them.

During the early evening of the 17th, Stavelot was virtually unoccupied. The only Americans in the town were in transit. In Malmedy, Dave Pergrin was still out on a limb. During the afternoon his C Company had arrived to reinforce him. Its commander, Captain Larry Moyer, had left a squad of men, under Sergeant Chuck Hensel, at Stavelot, with orders to mount a roadblock on the approach to the bridge. Later in the day Pergrin received welcome news – the 99th Norwegian Infantry Battalion, 526th Armoured Infantry Battalion and the 825th Tank Destroyer Battalion were all being dispatched to reinforce him in Malmedy. Pergrin advised that at least a company of the 526th, with some anti-tank guns from the 825th, should be sent immediately to Stavelot, although these would not arrive until the early hours of the next day.

On the hill above the bridge Sergeant Chuck Hensel set up his roadblock, with Private Bernie Goldstein some way further up the hill. Dave Pergrin takes up the story:

> *Shortly after Hensel had set up his roadblock on a narrow, curving road with a high rock cliff on the right, and a 100 foot drop-off on the left, the 13 man squad heard the sound of approaching tanks. In the darkness Private Bernie Goldstein, out on point, yelled 'Halt!' with only a rifle in his hand. All hell broke loose! Weapons fired, but the curve in the road protected Hensel and his men. Goldstein managed to escape up over the face of the cliff and head into the woods.*

The foundations of the building that stood at the point where Private Bernie Goldstein stood guard and challenged the kampfgruppe as it approached Stavelot on the night of 17 December 1944.

A King Tiger from Kampfgruppe Peiper passes a column of American prisoners.

As Hensel moved towards the area where Goldstein had been positioned, the Germans opened up with machine-gun fire. Gadziola was able to take a look beyond the curve and saw a large tank cross-ways to the road and almost over the embankment. The darkness didn't prevent the Germans from opening fire.

Gadziola ducked back under cover and told Hensel that he could not see Goldstein. The firing ceased and Hensel and his men heard the German tanks move back up the hill. Hensel discussed the situation with his men, and they decided that they should leave their mines in position and move down the hill to the bridge. They knew that the 7th Armoured Division was moving west through Stavelot, and the 13 man squad had been trained to get in, accomplish the engineering mission, and get out – especially in situations like this where their weapons were insufficient to fight tanks and knock out German armour.

Peiper decided to wait until the following morning before he continued his advance. His lead tanks had been challenged and they did not know what was waiting around the bend. Many vehicle headlights could be seen passing through the town below. Peiper had had another frustrating day. Numerous delays had taken place and his kampfgruppe was spread over miles of narrow winding roads. His Tiger battalion had moved via a more southerly route, and would not catch up for some hours. Years later, Peiper summed up the reasons for his decision to halt on the hill above Stavelot:

> At 16:00 we reached the area of Stavelot, which was heavily defended. We could observe heavy traffic moving from Malmedy towards Stavelot and Stavelot itself seemed clogged up completely with several hundred trucks. That night we attempted to capture Stavelot but the terrain presented great difficulties. The only approach was the main road and the ground to the left of the road fell very sharply and to the right of the road rose very sharply [Peiper has these the wrong way round from the German perspective]. There was a short curve just at the entrance to Stavelot where several Sherman tanks and anti-tank guns were zeroed in. Thereupon we shelled Stavelot with heavy infantry howitzers and mortars, resulting in great confusion within the town and the destruction of several dumps. At 18:00 a counter-attack circled around a high hill 800 metres east of Stavelot and hit my column from the south. The counter-attack consisted entirely of infantry. After the counter-attack was repulsed, I committed more armoured infantry to attack Stavelot again. We approached the outskirts of the village but bogged down because of stubborn American resistance at the edge of Stavelot. We suffered fairly heavy losses, 25-30 casualties, from tank, anti-tank, mortar and rifle fire. Since I did not yet have sufficient infantry, I decided to wait for the arrival of more infantry.

Other than the shelling of Stavelot, there is little evidence to support most of the foregoing, particularly the presence of American tanks, anti-tank guns and infantry during the evening of the 17th. One of Peiper's Panther commanders drew a completely different conclusion from what they were seeing below them in Stavelot:

> We could see the lights of the vehicles and hear them. I had the impression that the Amis were withdrawing.

It is easy to understand why Peiper gave such an excuse for not pushing on through Stavelot. He had made an error of judgement and tried to excuse himself. Finally, Dave Pergrin sums up the situation admirably:

> Little did Peiper know that at this time the only American unit between his 1st SS spearheading armoured column and its objective, the Meuse River, was the C Company squad of the 291st Engineer Combat Battalion.

It would not be the last time that a small body of engineers would stop Peiper's drive for the Meuse.

Chapter Five

18 DECEMBER 1944: THOSE DAMNED ENGINEERS

During the night of 17/18 December Peiper reorganized his kampfgruppe. Obersturmführer Kremser's 1 Company and Obersturmführer Christ's 2 Company of Pz.Rgt 1, both equipped with Panthers, together with Hauptsturmführer Preuss's 10 Company from Pz.Gren.Rgt 2, would form the lead element. For the assault on the bridge they would be supported by the pioneers of 9 Company, Pz.Rgt 1, who were tasked with taking the approach to the bridge. The remaining two companies of Pz.Rgt 1, 6 and 7, both equipped with Mk IVs, would advance on another axis south of the Ambleve with the objective of securing the crossings at Trois Ponts.

While Peiper hesitated on the hill above Stavelot, American reinforcements reached the town. At Lieutenant Colonel Dave Pergrin's request, part of the reinforcements sent to him in Malmedy were diverted to Stavelot. These comprised of A Company, 526th Armoured Infantry, and 1st Platoon of A Company, 825th TD Battalion. This small task force was commanded by Major Paul Solis. On his arrival, at sometime between 02:00 and 03:00 hrs on the morning of the 18th, Solis contacted the only other American troops in the

General view of Stavelot from the road down which the kampfgruppe approached the town.

town, C Company of the 202nd Engineers, commanded by Lieutenant Joe Chinland. Chinland had been given orders to blow the Stavelot bridge, but had failed to do so. If he had carried out his orders it is difficult to see how Peiper could have made any further progress. Chinland had laid mines on the bridge, and left one platoon with a machine gun to cover it while the other two platoons were moved back into defensive positions around the town square, to the north of the bridge. Solis was informed that the engineers had placed two roadblocks on the approach roads to the south of the bridge, and it quickly became apparent that these needed reinforcing. Two platoons were dispatched, with two of the 825th's towed 3-inch anti-tank guns.

At sometime between 05:00 and 06:00 hrs the two American platoons collided with Jupp Diefenthal's advancing panzer grenadiers. Lieutenant Harry Willyard's 2nd Platoon advanced up the road towards the now-abandoned site of Sergeant Hensel's roadblock, while Lieutenant Jack Doherty's 1st Platoon covered the road to the south-east of the bridge. Both platoons were quickly driven back across the bridge by the advancing Germans, losing most of their half-tracks and the anti-tank guns in the process. Diefenthal's 11 Company used the enemy's confusion to try and seize the bridge, but were unsuccessful, with their company commander Heinz Tomhardt wounded and one of the platoon leaders killed. Although they had been driven back to the south bank 11 Company had given the pioneers of 9 Company time to ensure that the bridge was clear of demolition charges.

While 11 Company's panzer grenadiers clung to the houses to the south of the river, Peiper's panzers began an attack on the bridge at about 08:00. Rottenführer Eugen Zimmermann commanded the lead panzer:

> *Obersturmbannführer Peiper himself designated my panzer as the lead panzer through Stavelot. The attack was to take place early in the morning. The entire crew received exact instructions. A 9.2 anti-tank gun sat right on the left-hand curve! The best way to negotiate it was in fifth gear and then give it the gas. During the night we received further instructions: an Untersturmführer was supposed to be lying in the centre of the bridge. Was he killed, or only wounded? We didn't know. The bridge was secured, watch out for the Untersturmführer! My feeling was – my God! – we can't cross that! We were all awake at dawn. The morning slowly grew greyer and then the order arrived: 'Warm up the engines, then, driver, march!' We met no resistance, the anti-tank gun was there, damaged, and we drove onto the bridge. The Untersturmführer was not there, thank God! No sooner had we arrived when we were hit. The driver screamed into the microphone: 'The gas pedal is stuck – we're hit!' I saw an anti-tank gun behind the corner of a house, 'Open fire!' The 7.5 is onto it – miss! The cannon points up into the sky. Fifth gear. Give it gas. The trail of the anti-tank gun broke, falling onto our radio hatch and lay there. Again there was heavy firing from all sides. Things were looking up. The firing died out. I made it through Stavelot.*

Peiper used his mortars and artillery to cover the panzers' advance, but the Germans didn't have everything their own way. The two remaining tank destroyers from the 825th, both M-10s, had positioned themselves on high ground about 300 yards north of the river, from where they had a clear view of the German column lined up along the road waiting for the bridge to be cleared. The tank destroyers reportedly engaged and destroyed or damaged several German panzers, and this is supported by Unterscharführer Karl Wortmann, who commanded a flakpanzer in 10 Company (flak) of Pz.Rgt 1:

We were standing in a long column in the early morning hours. The small city of Stavelot lay before us in the valley. In order to be able to transit this town, we had to cross the narrow, stone Ambleve bridge. The Americans had committed all the heavy weapons available in Stavelot to protect this bridge. Several of our panzers lost a few feathers here. Worse was the fact that one of our Panthers was hit and blocked the narrow bridge access. We continued to attack to open the bridge. In the meantime, day had dawned. Visibility was clear and a portion of our panzer column, to which our two flakpanzers belonged, was well observed by the enemy. We had no opportunity to withdraw. The Americans blanketed us with fire from a variety of calibres. We crawled into every available cover. In the later morning the enemy resistance ebbed. It had cost us several panzers and wounded, but the bridge over the Ambleve was open.

Although the Americans were still resisting, the lead elements of the kampfgruppe began to flow through Stavelot, taking the road to the west towards the bridges at Trois Ponts. Peiper had his mind firmly set on his objectives:

Kampfgruppe Peiper's route, Stavelot to La Gleize, 18 December 1944.

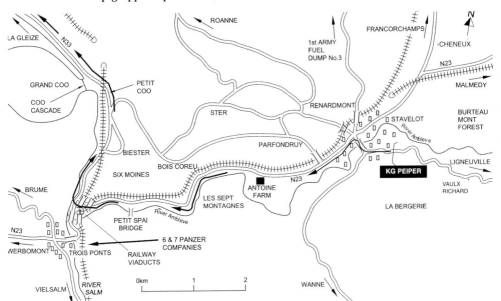

When we penetrated Stavelot, too many civilians shot at us from the windows and openings in their roofs. The only goal that I was looking for was the bridge near Trois Ponts. I, therefore, had no time to spend on those civilians and continued driving on, although I knew that resistance in this town had not been decisively broken.

Peiper's mission was to drive hard for the Meuse, and follow-up troops could see to the remaining enemy at Stavelot. American troops continued to fire on the passing Germans for between half an hour and an hour. Solis realized that until further support arrived he could not hold the town, and withdrew up the Francorchamps road, along which was a massive fuel dump. Realizing that the Germans could be close on his heels, Solis ordered his men to set fire to the dump, then dug in to the north of it. The burning fuel dump has been cited as the cause for Peiper heading west towards Trois Ponts, and Captain Franklin Ferriss, Historical Officer with 30th Division, reported:

A column of enemy armour, estimated by one observer to consist of at least 15 vehicles, advanced up the road from Stavelot as far as the burning gasoline.

It is difficult to identify who these Germans were, if indeed a German column ever approached the dump, as Kampfgruppe Peiper did not move up the Francorchamps road, but headed west towards Trois Ponts.

As the kampfgruppe's vehicles passed through Stavelot their machine guns were fired at any threat. This building still shows the scars.

At 11:00 hrs the lead element of the kampfgruppe approached Trois Ponts, with its precious bridges. As the road from Stavelot approached the town the lead tank was engaged by an enemy anti-tank gun, as its commander Eugen Zimmermann reports:

We came upon the railroad, the order 'sharp left' came over the radio. At that moment we were hit, but, thank God, it was only a graze. Apparently, we were moving too fast. I was able to exactly recognize the anti-tank gun and aimed the cannon, not with the optics, but directly through the barrel, at a stone wall immediately behind the anti-tank gun. One high-explosive shell and there was no more resistance. We cautiously negotiated the underpass. I thought for sure there would be another anti-tank gun. It was quiet! But the bridge on the left was blown. Sturmbannführer Poetschke and Obersturmbannführer Peiper approached on foot to see what the problem was. Then to the right! Halt! One hundred metres ahead was a pile of mines, 4x5 metres and 1.5 metres high, directly on the road! It was impossible to bypass, for, if we were blown up, our panzer would block the entire road. We radioed: 'Irmgard, this is Carbid, over' – again and again – no reply! The railroad embankment was too steep for the UHF frequency transmitter. I decided to aim the cannon through the tube at the middle of the explosives! Closed all hatches! Fire! The pile of mines blew into the air with an extra-ordinary explosion. We continued the advance.

The two railway underpasses on the approaches to Trois Ponts. It was close to this spot that Peiper's lead tank was engaged by an American anti-tank gun, which it destroyed.

Trois Ponts was held by a small number of American engineers, and again it was these who frustrated Peiper's advance. Private Audrus Salazar formed part of a 51st ECB roadblock, close to the anti-tank gun destroyed by Eugen Zimmermann. Salazar, although wounded, was able to reach the Ambleve bridge with a warning that the Germans were approaching, and the bridge was promptly blown.

Peiper had hoped to return to the main Werbomont road through Trois Ponts, from where he could push on to the River Lienne, and then on to the Meuse. From his overnight position, on the hill overlooking Stavelot, two routes ran to Trois Ponts, where they joined before continuing on to the west. The first route was that taken by the main body of the kampfgruppe – across the Ambleve bridge, through Stavelot. The second route ran south from Stavelot to Wanne, and then turned west to Trois Ponts, and it was along this road that Peiper ordered the Mk IVs of Pz.Rgt 1's 6 and 7 Companies to proceed, accompanied by pioneers and some of the 9th Fallschirmjager Regiment men still with the kampfgruppe.

The kampfgruppe emerged from the railway underpasses where the car is at the junction opposite the Ford Dealer. Peiper's intention was to turn left (south) towards Trois Ponts, but the bridge had been blown. Instead the kampfgruppe turned right (north) and followed the N633 towards La Gleize.

The N66 bridge over the Ambleve at Trois Ponts. This bridge was blown minutes before the leading elements of the kampfgruppe emerged from the underpass (behind the photographer).

The Salm River bridge at Trois Ponts. This bridge was blown in the face of 6 and 7 Companies of Panzer Regiment 1 by members of the 51st Engineer Combat Battalion on 18 December 1944. (*Airborne Forces Museum*)

C Company of the 51st ECB had set up a roadblock covering the road from Wanne on the heights above the Salm River. They engaged the leading Mk IVs with bazookas, but were unsuccessful, and the engineers quickly withdrew back across the river. At 13:00 hrs Colonel Anderson, commander of the 1111th Engineer Group, ordered Lieutenant 'Bucky' Walters, 51st ECB, to blow the Salm bridge. The Mk IVs were descending the road from the heights when they saw the bridge explode into the air. They would not pass through Trois Ponts that day, or any other. Not only had the bridge been blown in their faces, but they were also virtually out of fuel. It would take several days for fuel to reach them, by which time they would be needed for the continued fighting at Stavelot.

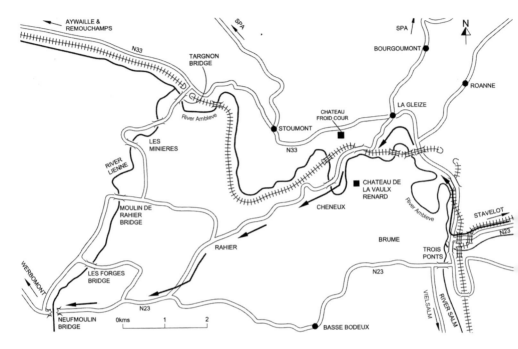

Kampfgruppe Peiper's route, La Gleize to Neufmoulin bridge, 18 December 1944.

After the Ambleve bridge had been blown Peiper had no choice but to continue north along the river to La Gleize. From here he had two choices. First, he could cross the Ambleve, continue through Cheneux, and rejoin the Werbomont road to the east of the Lienne. This would put him back on his preferred route. The second option was to continue along the Ambleve through Stoumont. Peiper decided on the first course of action, and his column proceeded through La Gleize and almost to Cheneux without any interference from the enemy. At 13:00 hrs the cloud cover cleared and an American reconnaissance aircraft spotted the kampfgruppe. For the next two hours Peiper's men were subjected to heavy air attack by elements of the IX TAC (Tactical Air Command), although the flakpanzers put up a brave fight. Karl Wortmann's flakpanzer was heavily involved in trying to drive off the American fighter-bombers:

> The cloudy and overcast winter weather had somewhat broken and the sun shone for a moment. The march formation was located on a narrow mountain road and stretched for 2km. A long rocky wall stretched along the right side of the road, falling off steeply into the valley. When 16 Thunderbolts attacked them from one side of the valley, the vehicles stood without cover on the long stretch. There wasn't the slightest chance of them to withdraw. The panzer crews and

the grenadiers crawled into or under their steel colossi, a defenceless and powerless offering on a silver platter. The two flakpanzers immediately opened fire with their four-barrelled weapons and let go with all they had. However, the 'violinists of the air' attacked piteously, firing their on-board weapons and dropping bombs. It was hopeless for the men in the flakpanzers against 16 aircraft. They could not concentrate on one aircraft because too many were attacking at once. They blazed away in a general manner at one-and-all, made the pilots unsure and prevented the enemy from accurately engaging their targets. The amount of rounds spit out by the eight barrels was enormous, as was indicated by the flak clouds. The men on the two guns ignored the sweat on their faces and the anxiety in their throats as they were continuously attacked by the aircraft. Their panzer turrets turned lightning-fast to the right and to the left, as required, in order to drive off the enemy aircraft. One Thunderbolt was set ablaze by the flakpanzer guns, falling out of the sky several seconds later. After half an hour, when the enemy aircraft veered off, Obersturmbannführer Peiper thanked the men in the flakpanzers.

The approach to Cheneux from La Gleize. The Ambleve Bridge can be seen towards the left of the photograph. It was along this stretch of road that the kampfgruppe was attacked by American fighter-bombers.

A German column under attack from American fighter-bombers. The kampfgruppe suffered such an attack on the afternoon of 18 December 1944, close to Cheneux.
(*Airborne Forces Museum*)

Although the flak crews did their utmost to protect the column, Peiper lost three Panthers and five SPWs, along with a number of dead and wounded. By the time the kampfgruppe had cleared the road, and tended to their dead and wounded, another three hours had been lost. This gave time for American engineers to prepare the Lienne bridge for destruction.

The kampfgruppe continued down the road from Cheneux to Rahier, and beyond to the main Werbomont road, the N23. Obersturmführer Flacke, Jupp Diefenthal's adjutant, was with the lead panzers as they began to approach the bridge:

> *Behind Rahier, I ran into the main Trois Ponts – Werbomont road fork. A panzer from I Battalion and an SPW from III Battalion stood in front of this fork. I continued the advance with the panzers and reached the forest exit about 1,000 metres in front of the bridge over Lienne near Neucy. Shortly, thereafter, the bridge was blown, bringing our attack to a halt. We turned back, forced to reconnoitre a new crossing over the river.*

Staff Sergeant Edwin Pigg was platoon sergeant of 2nd Platoon, A Company, 291st ECB. He was tasked by his platoon leader, Lieutenant Edelstein, with preparing the Lienne bridge at Habiemont for demolition. Pigg gathered ten men, mainly from the 3rd squad, and departed by truck from Werbomont for the bridge at 13:30 hrs, arriving there at 15:00. Pigg and his men immediately began to prepare the bridge, attaching explosive charges to all the bridge piers, connected by primacord. They also prepared a second charge just in case the first one failed. The American engineers had some warning that the Germans were approaching. Firstly, they could see American fighter-bombers attacking something in the distance. Secondly, two local Belgians had arrived at the bridge and warned them that a large German armoured column was approaching. At 16:45 hrs the German column hove into view, and the commanding officer of the 291st ECB, Dave Pergrin, takes up the story:

> *At 4:45 p.m. about midway into the evening's period of dusk, Corporal Chapin spotted the first German tank as it nosed out of the gloom about 200 yards east of the demolition prepared bridge.*

> *The Engineers were ready, even with a second charge should the first charge fail. So were the Germans. The gunner of the lead Royal Tiger saw activity on the bridge and opened fire with his main gun. The engineers ducked in every direction. The detonator left in the open was grabbed by Corporal Chapin who looked for a signal from Edelstein, and as the platoon commander waved his arms, Chapin let her go. 2,500 pounds of TNT sent the timber trestle flying in bits and pieces in all directions!*

> *In complete dismay, Colonel Peiper shouted 'Those damned Engineers. Those damned Engineers!' All of this in the din of the explosion of the bridge. Peiper saw the dream of reaching the Meuse River disappearing in front of him. The leading Tiger Royals approached the bridge and opened fire with their machine guns at the engineers as they raced for their truck. Corporal Chapin, who was nearest to the machine-gun fire, was the last to make the truck but all the*

The approach to the Lienne Bridge along the N66. At last light on 18 December 1944 the bridge was blown by a squad from A Company, 291st ECB, as the Germans approached. It is at this point that Peiper is reported to have exclaimed 'Those damned engineers!'

'damned Engineers' made it safely. They were able to stay overnight with the advance party of the 82nd Airborne at Werbomont and return to their company headquarters on the morning of the 19th of December.

Not all Peiper's options had disappeared. He dispatched part of Hauptsturmführer Preuss's 10 Company to reconnoitre a bridge to the north to see if it would take the weight of his tanks. Preuss's men crossed the bridge and turned south, moving down the west side of the river towards the Habiemont bridge. Another of the 'damned Engineers' was lying in wait for them. Private Johnny Rondenell had been sent about 300 yards up the road north from the Habiemont bridge, and had laid a 'daisy chain' mine roadblock. Sometime after the bridge had been blown, and his fellow engineers had departed, Rondenell heard vehicles approaching from the north:

I heard the sound of approaching vehicles that sounded like half-tracks and I felt that the daisy chain mines would do the job. However the first half-track passed through the mines and nothing happened. Soon a second light half-track did the same. At this time I felt concerned that these German vehicles were on their way into the American defenses.

I then pulled the mines to the west about 2 feet and didn't have long to wait. I moved back further into the woods and soon heard a large explosion as the recon vehicle flipped completely over. I then made a hurried retreat back into the woods. I then started to head back towards Habiemont, but found myself lost in the deep woods. I don't know how long I was lost but a few hours later I found the site where we blew the bridge. There were two knocked out German recon vehicles there and a number of dead German soldiers. I worked my way back to Werbomont and found the 82nd Airborne troops arriving.

Lieutenant Colonel Hal McCown's 2nd Battalion, 119th IR, 30th Division, had arrived in the area of the Habiemont bridge at sometime between when it had been blown and 22:00 hrs, when Preuss's company arrived at the bridge. Captain Franklin Ferriss reports the ensuing contact:

Company F's commander, Lieutenant Edward C. Arn, dispersed his men and the two M-10s made available to him. He had just finished placing the forward TD [tank destroyer] gun into position, and the infantrymen along the side of the road were still digging their foxholes, when at about 22:00 hours, five enemy half-tracks passed the house occupied by Lieutenant Austin's platoon. The leading half-track mounted a 75mm assault gun which fired two rounds into this house, and so stunned Lieutenant Austin's men, that they retired to the cellar. The column of half-tracks proceeded on up the road. Not a shot was fired at it until the lead half-track approached to within 40 yards of the first TD gun. The driver of the lead half-track at this point flicked on his headlights, apparently in order to make out a bend in the road. Instantly, the TD gun put three rounds into this half-track, which went up in flames and lit up the whole area. The American soldiers on the sides of the road and in the first house passed by the enemy column, then opened up with all available weapons. One of the remaining half-tracks was knocked out while it was attempting to make a U-turn. Another one was abandoned. The remaining two managed to turn around, but were stopped by bazooka fire as they passed the house occupied by Lieutenant Austin's platoon. One prisoner taken identified the half-tracks as belonging to the 2nd Panzer Grenadier Regiment. The enemy made no further effort to break through Company F's roadblock that night or prior to 2nd Battalion's relief by the 82nd Airborne Division at 15:30 19 December.

It is interesting that Ferriss reports five half-tracks being destroyed, while Rondenell reported seeing only two. It is possible that Rondenell saw only the last two, which had been knocked out while trying to withdraw. He also does not report seeing any American troops in the area of the bridge, although F Company was definitely in the area until late afternoon on the following day. One last report of this incident comes from Hauptsturmführer Preuss himself:

The 10th Company was committed to quickly advance against Werbomont. The advance moved through Rahier-Froidville-Chaudveheid-Forges-Habiemont. Apparently because of an incorrect location report and believing that we were still within our own security belt, we fell into an American armoured ambush near Outry and suffered heavy casualties.

Preuss retraced his route with the remainder of his company. He reported to Peiper that the bridge would take SPWs, but would not support tanks. Peiper's way along the Werbomont road was now firmly blocked. During the remainder of the night and the early hours of the 19th, the kampfgruppe returned to La Gleize, having left a small garrison in Cheneux to protect the flank of their march route. During this retreat Karl Wortmann and his crew ran into trouble:

We drove back in the direction of La Gleize. The night was very cloudy and literally we could not make anything out. We had already passed through the town of Rahier and the small village of Cheneux. Soon we had again come upon the large viaduct. Suddenly, in a left curve our panzer broke down. What was wrong? Even my experienced Erich Miechen was struck speechless. All of the other panzers overtook us. Then we were all alone on a wide stretch. The maintenance panzer was already towing another panzer. He would come back for us later! As time passed it became quite uncomfortable. We stood alone in the night and waited. The morning soon dawned. Then we suddenly heard tracked vehicles behind us. What were we to do? We stood like a target on a firing range! Our driver, Gunther Strater, set up the machine gun. My crew took up position behind the enormous pillars of the viaduct. The noise of the tracks grew louder and at any moment they would have to appear from behind the last houses of Cheneux. They had to be Americans, because everyone else had passed us. Then the first one appeared from behind a house, the second tank was immediately behind it, then, after a distance, the third and fourth. They were driving slowly, almost at walking speed, they were extremely cautious. They slowly closed the distance to our panzer. I observed quite closely that each two advanced close together. One was towing the other! Soon I recognized them as German panzers. Konigstigers from our 501st Heavy Battalion! I ran up and stopped them. Then I recognized one of the commanders, it was Hauptsturmführer Mobius. These Konigstigers, like our panzer column, had been on the road continuously since the first day of the attack. They were almost out of fuel. They had emptied the fuel tanks of two panzers so that the other two could continue. That was why they were towing them!

Fuel problems had already struck Peiper's Mk IV companies near Wanne. Now they would come to haunt the remainder of the kampfgruppe. In the morning the advance would continue along the Stoumont road to the west of La Gleize.

In Stavelot, elements of the kampfgruppe and Schnellgruppe Knittel had continued to pass through the town throughout the day. Not all the Germans had passed through the town unscathed. Obersturmführer Jurgen Wessel, commander of 1 Company, 501st Heavy Panzer Battalion, led his company's King Tigers through the town:

The main body of Kampfgruppe Peiper, the 2nd Company and battalion staff had already passed through Stavelot when I approached the town with the 1st Company. I myself drove point. I took a hit shortly before reaching the Ambleve

SS Panzergrenadiers pause for a cigarette during their advance.
(Airborne Forces Museum)

bridge. Cannon no longer operational I drove at high speed across the bridge and soon came upon a rectangular square where we were hit by two anti-tank rounds on the bow. I backed up my panzer into a house wall, which collapsed, on top of my vehicle. Then my crew and I bailed out from under the panzer. I set the next panzer following of my company, Oberscharführer Brand, to take on the enemy anti-tank gun while I climbed into the next panzer. With this panzer I took off at high speed through Stavelot in order to find contacts forward. However, my company could no longer follow and I could not return, since the Americans had reinforced themselves in the town. Even later, the company was not able to regain contact with Kampfgruppe Peiper.

It is possible that Wessel's Tiger is the same one that Captain Franklin Ferriss reported being engaged by infantry from the newly arrived 1st Battalion, 117th Infantry:

Sometime before midnight a German tank rolled up to the square in the middle of the town that constituted a 'no man's land'. Bazooka and AT grenades persuaded the tank crew to put it in reverse. It backed into a building and the building collapsed on the tank. The crew was forced to abandon it. A second tank was knocked out by bazooka and AT grenade fire about a block the other side of the square. There were two more tanks behind it, but on account of the narrowness of the street, they could not move or even fire past the knocked-out tank.

A second German source, one of Wessel's panzer commanders, Oberscharführer Wendt, also reports this incident:

Wessel climbed to the second panzer and drove along the street which turned in the direction of Trois Ponts before the market. Brand was about 30m behind the bridge, stalled. I could not pass him because of the narrow street and my 3.75m wide panzer. Therefore, we helped him repair his track. Meanwhile it had become dark. Since we had lost all contact with forward and rear, we decided to wait the day. Nothing more happened until about midnight when a burst of flak passed us.

With the exception of the time of day the three accounts tell a similar story. As Wessel's Tiger approached the square it was engaged by anti-tank weapons, but was unable to reply due to the damage to its gun, received while crossing the bridge. The Tiger reversed clear of the square, but backed into a building, which collapsed on it. Wessel called Brand forward to engage the enemy, and his tank was also engaged, and lost a track. By this time Wessel had mounted another panzer and continued out of the town towards Trois Ponts. Unfortunately, the rest of his company were unable to follow him.

Schnellgruppe Knittel was formed around Gustav Knittel's 1st Aufklarungsabteilung (Armoured Reconnaissance Battalion). Knittel was originally tasked to follow Kampfgruppe Hansen along Route E. Due to delays on Route E he was ordered to transfer onto Route D, as Kampfgruppe Peiper had broken through the American lines and was pushing on through Stavelot. Knittel's 2nd Company arrived at Stavelot at about midday, and one of its members reported the problems they had passing through the town:

The 2nd Company reached the town of Stavelot at midday. It led the battalion. Shortly before reaching the first houses, we received artillery fire. We had to dismount and cross the city on foot. Shortly after midday, between 12:00 hrs and 13:00 hrs, we reached the western edge of Stavelot. There we again received artillery fire. We stayed there alone on the western edge. No other companies followed. Our SPWs drove along the road west of Stavelot. As we started out an American air attack occurred. I also saw the aircraft attack the road east of Stavelot, where the other companies of the battalion had to be located. The attack lasted until shortly before the fall of darkness. Then we mounted and drove on.

It was not only Peiper's column at Cheneux that received the attention of the American fighter-bombers once the cloudy skies cleared. Contrary to the previous quote, 2 Company was not the only company of Knittel's unit that reached the western edge of Stavelot. The bulk of the battalion, including 3 Company, also passed through the town, and was involved in an attempt to attack American artillery positions in the wooded terrain to the west of Stavelot, as a member of the company, Helmut Merscher, recorded:

Today we had to go through Stavelot, which was burning in many locations. We had no chance of riding our bicycles through the city. We loaded up onto trucks and were driven through the city, firing to the left and right. We were taking heavy casualties from American artillery, which was set in positions west of the city in a forest. We were now supposed to attack and destroy these positions. We set up our command post in a farmhouse directly in the forest. My squad, under Unterscharführer Pries, advanced as the first scout element. We found no guns, but a group of Americans who were enjoying God's good graces in warm bunkers. There were three bunkers without guards at the entrances. We attacked with three men against each bunker and threw hand-grenades inside through the stovepipes!

The attack was led by Obersturmführer Leidreiter, but when the American guns could not be found, the elements of Schnellgruppe Knittel that had passed through Stavelot continued their march to La Gleize, where they met the main body of Kampfgruppe Peiper as it arrived back from its abortive attempt to capture the Lienne bridge at Habiemont.

During the 18th a large proportion of the kampfgruppe had crossed the bridge at Stavelot and ended the day at La Gleize. The Panthers of 1 and 2 Companies of Pz.Rgt 1 and at least seven Tigers had reached La Gleize, together with Diefenthal's panzer grenadier battalion. Other units with the kampfgruppe at the end of the day were Rumpf's 9 Panzer Pioneer Company and a number of flak vehicles from von Sacken's 84th Luftwaffe Flak Battalion. Five Mk IVs from 6 Company had managed to reach Peiper, after draining the fuel tanks of the remaining tanks in the 6 and 7 Companies. Several other Tigers and a Panther spent the night in Stavelot before moving to rejoin the kampfgruppe on the 19th. These tanks were taken under command by Knittel who had been ordered to keep the route through Stavelot clear. Although some of the kampfgruppe were still south of the

An American column moves up under difficult conditions to help stem the German breakthrough.

Ambleve, Peiper had a powerful force at his command, and would continue his drive on the following day.

On the American side, moves were afoot to halt the German breakthrough. Two veteran divisions began to move into the area. The first of these, 30th Infantry Division, came into contact with elements of Peiper's force at Habiemont and Stavelot during the 18th. The 30th moved from its assembly areas to the north of Aachen to Eupen in Belgium on 17 December. Its 117th Regiment, supported by the 118th Field Artillery Battalion, was dispatched to reinforce the Malmedy area. The 117th's commander, Colonel Walter Johnson, decided to move his 3rd Battalion into Malmedy, while his 2nd Battalion covered the Ambleve between Malmedy and Stavelot. His 1st Battalion, under Lieutenant Colonel Robert Frankland, carried on to Stavelot.

Frankland was reinforced with two reconnaissance platoons, a tank destroyer platoon, and three 75mm self-propelled guns. He also had the promise of at least one platoon of M-4 Sherman tanks. The battalion debussed to the north of the fuel dump on the Francorchamps road, and advanced on the town with a company leading on each side of the road. Initially, the battalion had no artillery support, but during the afternoon the 118th Field Artillery Battalion got into position. The battalion had been delayed by the attack of part of Schnellgruppe Knittel, and had moved to avoid the attack. Later in the day this support was reinforced by the 113th Field Artillery Battalion.

Frankland's battalion was opposed by limited tank and infantry fire from Stavelot, which did little to stop their drive towards the town. By nightfall the 1/117th had occupied the northern half of Stavelot. Lieutenant Ellis McInnis's platoon of C Company, 823rd TD Battalion, provided Frankland with valuable fire support, and engaged the enemy on the south bank of the Ambleve, knocking out several panzers and SPWs. Frankland received a further reinforcement of three Shermans from B Company of the 743rd Tank Battalion. By midnight the 1st Battalion had established contact with the 2nd Battalion to the east of Stavelot. Unfortunately, Frankland's right flank was in the air and open to attack from the west. The Germans carried out a couple of probing attacks against the 1st Battalion positions, both of which were quickly

SS troops pause during the drive weatward.

halted, and at this they left Frankland's men alone for the remainder of the night.

The other unit of the 30th Division to contact the enemy on the 18th was Hal McCown's 2/119th. F Company's clash with Preuss's 10 Company has already been described. On the 19th McCown's unit would be relieved by the 82nd Airborne Division, which had also left its assembly area at Camps Suippes and Sissonne in France to help stem the German attack. The Divisional Commander, General Jim Gavin, in his post action report describes his arrival in the area of Peiper's drive:

> I arrived at Werbomont at approximately mid-afternoon and immediately made a reconnaissance of the entire area. It offered excellent defensive possibilities, being the dominant terrain for many miles from the crossroads at Werbomont. At about 16:00 hrs I contacted an engineer platoon at the bridge at Habiemont [the squad from Lieutenant Edelstein's platoon]. The bridge was prepared for demolition and they reported the Germans were in the immediate vicinity, coming over the main highway from Trois Ponts. At that time a number of civilians were very excitedly moving west on the Trois Ponts-Werbomont road. They all stated that the Germans had passed Trois Ponts and were 'coming this way'. I made a reconnaissance down the valley from Habiemont to the Ambleve River but encountered no enemy or any indication of his whereabouts. One bridge was still in tact at Forge and was not prepared for demolition. Upon returning to Habiemont I asked the Lieutenant [Edelstein] at that bridge about it, but he appeared to be fully occupied with the means at his disposal of blowing the bridge at Habiemont. At about 16:30 hrs I left for Bastogne to meet General McAuliffe.

Gavin missed the arrival of Peiper's column by fifteen minutes! The first elements of his division arrived in Werbomont at 20:00 hrs. Although Peiper was still set on driving for the Meuse the next day, his enemies were closing upon him in force.

Chapter Six

19 DECEMBER 1944:
FURTHEST POINT

While Peiper gathered his forces in La Gleize an American infantry battalion had arrived at Stoumont to block his road to the west. Lieutenant Colonel Roy Fitzgerald's 3rd Battalion of the 119th IR reached Stoumont after dark on the 18th, and immediately occupied defensive positions in the town. Fitzgerald had been reinforced by eight towed anti-tank guns, probably 3-inch-calibre, from A Company, 823rd TD Battalion. He also had two 90mm anti-aircraft guns from the 143rd AAA Gun Battalion, in addition to three 57mm anti-tank guns belonging to battalion HQ. Fitzgerald deployed his three rifle companies along the edge of the town. I Company, with four 3-inch anti-tank guns, covered the road from La Gleize, and a minefield was hastily laid in front of their positions. K Company, with the remaining four 3-inch anti-tank guns, deployed along the south edge of the town, while L Company, with the battalion's three 57mm anti-tank guns, deployed on the north side of the town, in a small suburb called Rouat.

Fitzgerald's battalion was not in a particularly good position. All three rifle companies were under strength, and no armour or artillery support was available. His troops had deployed after dark, and had no real idea of the lie

Defensive position of 3/119th and KG Peiper's advance, 19 December 1944.

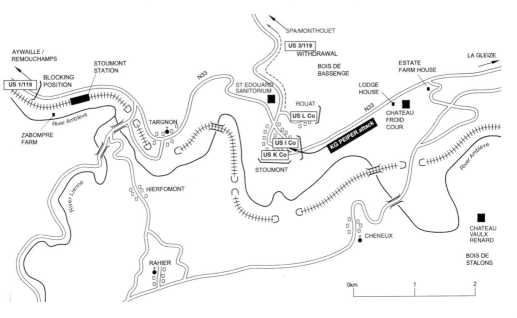

Panthers from Kampfgruppe Peiper approaching Stoumont on the morning of 19 December 1944. The lead tank is on fire after receiving a direct hit.

of the land. It was known that an enemy armoured column lay to the east in La Gleize, but the land suited an armoured attack as it was open to both sides of the La Gleize road. The commanding officer of the 119th IR, Colonel Sutherland, had requested armoured support from 30th Division, and had been promised a company.

The first German move came at about 03:00 hrs, when a reconnaissance vehicle hit a mine in front of I Company's position. At 06:45 the Germans began a mortar bombardment, which was a prelude to their main attack. At 07:00 the first German attack came in. Through the early morning fog came six Panthers from Obersturmführer Christ's 2 Company, accompanied by two of 6 Company's Mk IVs. The panzers were supported by elements of both Untersturmführer Leike's and Obersturmführer Rumpf's pioneer companies, together with the remaining fallschirmjagers, which Peiper had picked up at Lanzerath three days earlier. The pioneers and fallschirmjagers advanced on foot through the woods to the south of the road. Following these lead elements were Oberscharführer Rudi Rayer's 11 Company and Oberscharführer Pfalzer's cannon platoon of 12 Company. Both companies belonged to Panzer Grenadier Regiment 2. Several batteries of I Battalion Panzer Artillery Regiment 1 had managed to transit through Stavelot, and would provide the advance with artillery support from their positions around La Gleize. Bob Hall, Headquarters Company, 3rd Battalion 119th IR, had been sent out towards La Gleize to watch for a German advance:

> *The Germans were in the next town, La Gleize. Lieutenant Goodman sent me, Ellis 'Jim' Aldridge, from Hagerstown, Maryland, who had been right next to me both times when I was wounded, and a third guy to a hilly area to observe any movement. When dawn broke, we could see what looked like the whole German army coming, infantry and tanks.*

Although the German force Hall glimpsed through the fog was only Peiper's advance guard, it must have seemed a massive force to the three men stuck out beyond the lines on their own.

The reduced visibility allowed the attacking panzers to approach the eastern edge of Stoumont almost undetected, and the engineers and fallschirmjagers were able to overrun the first American anti-tank guns on the eastern edge of the town. This was the signal for the remaining American anti-tank guns to open fire. Due to the closeness of their targets the effect on the impetus of the attack was devastating, and when an American 90mm anti-

Sturmbannführer Werner Poetschke, commander of the 1st Battalion, Panzer Regiment 1, in action at Stoumont.

aircraft gun positioned near Stoumont church also opened fire the attack began to show signs of grinding to a halt. It took Sturmbannführer Werner Poetschke's personal intervention to urge Obersturmführer Christ forward again, but the panzers advanced despite the anti-tank and infantry flanking fire that was now raining down on the leading tanks, which included Panther 223 commanded by Rottenführer Franz Prahm, whose gunner, Hans-Georg Hubler, described what followed:

> We took several hits from anti-tank guns one after the other from the direction of the church. This jammed our turret. While I was trying to aim our gun at the anti-tank gun, despite the jamming, we were hit in the engine compartment by an anti-tank gun shell from the left. Then the tank began to burn.

Prahm ordered his crew to bail out into the inferno of fire that surrounded them. Poetschke was still in the thick of things, urging the attack forward whenever, and wherever it looked like stalling. Peiper would recommend him for the award of Oak Leaves to his Knight's Cross, and wrote in the recommendation:

> The attack, which had been initiated immediately, soon came to a standstill when the road was effectively blocked by fire from four anti-tank/anti-aircraft guns and six heavy anti-tank guns on the outskirts of the village as well as enemy tanks in the woods on the northern edge of Stoumont. In clear recognition of the fact that a bold advance would have success, even at the cost of material, Poetschke placed himself at the head of his tanks and swept them forward through his example. Despite that, the attack did not succeed and a few vehicles began to pull back slowly in order to reach the cover of the protective reverse slope of a hill. At this moment of crisis, Poetschke was gripped with a towering rage. He climbed out of his tank, grabbed a panzerfaust and threatened to knock out his own tank crews who would roll a single step to the rear. This brutal measure was decisive. Disregarding the murderous fire and their own casualties, the tanks penetrated into the town – firing wildly – caused a great panic and broke the stiff resistance. 150 prisoners, 4 anti-tank/anti-aircraft guns, 5 heavy anti-tank guns, 4 Shermans as well as a lot of war material and enemy dead fell into our hands.

Captain Franklin Ferriss sums up the German attack from the American viewpoint:

> Two initial enemy assaults by infantry supported by tank fire were repulsed. Then five tanks moved against Company I's positions, while the same number simultaneously hit Company L on the north. At this time, it was still not very light, and on this account and because of an early morning fog, the gunners on the first two TD guns lost the lead tank in their sights. Without running into any of the mines that had been set out, the column of tanks advanced beyond the position of the first two TDs and the foxholes of the supporting infantry without being fired upon. The 3rd TD gun fired four rounds at the lead tank, all of which ricocheted. This gun was quickly knocked out by enemy 88mm fire [more likely 75mm fire from the Panthers]. One of the crew was killed and all the

Stoumont. The kampfgruppe's attack became stalled by anti-tank fire from the lower part of the village. It was in the area to the lower left of the photograph that Werner Poetschke was photographed retrieving a panzerfaust to assist the attack.

rest wounded. The crew of the fourth TD gun supporting Company I was picked off by German infantry.

Without any protection from the German panzers, I Company were forced to withdraw into the centre of the town, under covering fire of Lieutenant Walter Macht's tanks and one of the 90mm anti-aircraft guns. Macht, C Company, 743rd Tank Battalion, had arrived with ten tanks about 30 minutes after the first German attack. Four had been sent to support I Company, and four to L Company at Rouat. The remaining two Shermans were held in reserve. Macht continued to engage the German infantry and tanks, holding them up for a further two hours, reportedly 'disabling five German tanks, destroying three half-tracks, and causing many enemy casualties, without suffering a single casualty themselves'. This seems at odds with Peiper, who reported the destruction of four Shermans.

Members of the 3rd Battalion, 119th Infantry Regiment, surrendering at Stoumont. Most of these men were freed when the Americans occupied La Gleize on the morning of 24 December 1944.

After two hours the American forces began to withdraw from the town, towards the north and west. By 10:00 hrs I and K Companies had pulled back to the north of the town, while L Company and Macht's tanks moved back towards Stoumont station. Lieutenant David Fox, commanding L Company, had used a smokescreen, created by white phosphorous grenades, to cover his withdrawal. Lieutenant Macht's tanks had more of a problem, as the first 500 yards of their withdrawal along the road towards Stoumont station was over open ground. Macht split his tanks into two groups of five, one of which covered the withdrawal of the other. The first group then withdrew under the cover of the other's guns. Both groups managed to fall back without any losses.

Jochen Peiper was in the thick of the fighting in Stoumont:

As there was still heavy firing on that side, I stopped at the first house on the left. An American anti-tank gun was located next to the house and a burning Panther. From that I concluded that it would take a while to mop up in the city. First I wanted to establish a contact point in the house. A few officers of my staff, as well as Poetschke, von Westernhagen and Nuske, came over to where I was, as did my signals officer. Then I saw an American medic standing at the house with his back against the door. As there were still a couple of American dead and wounded lying on the ground, and as the surroundings didn't seem to be especially safe, I gestured to the medic to come over and asked him a couple of questions as to whether there were still any Americans in the house or nearby houses. Then I went to an American anti-aircraft position near the house to see if these weapons were still usable.

When I returned there was such a heavy artillery barrage that I had to take cover. In this case, that meant that I jumped into the back of the house. But as the incoming rounds were very close, I came back out and lay down on the other side under the window. There I found my adjutant and a couple of men who had also taken cover. I ordered my adjutant to set up a command post at some distance from the house, as the artillery had zeroed in too well on this position. Then I climbed into his jeep with Sturmbannführer Poetschke and drove through Stoumont.

I met Hauptsturmführer Diefenthal on the west side of the city and ordered him to immediately push on after the retiring enemy forces and, under no circumstances, was he to allow any vehicle to stop, but to press on with all speed.

Before 12:00 hrs, the leading panzers and the panzer grenadiers of 11 Company were off in pursuit of the Americans withdrawing towards the west, after pioneers removed American mines from the road. Oberscharführer Walter Ropeter's Panther '225' of 2 Company, Pz. Rgt 1, was the point tank, as the advance guard of the kampfgruppe pushed on through Targnon village towards Stoumont station, 3 kilometres to the west of Stoumont. The Americans were in disarray. The only troops in Peiper's path were Lieutenant Macht's tanks, which were very low on ammunition, and a few infantrymen.

PzKfw V Ausf. G 'Panther'

Panzerkampfwagen Mk V Panther. Designed after the German army's shock of coming up against the Russian T34.

Crew:	5
Weight:	45 tons
Speed:	34 mph
Main gun:	75mm KwK 42 L70
Machine guns:	3 x 7.92mm MG
Maximum armour:	110mm

The Panther was designed to combat the Russian T34-series tanks, and incorporated many similar design features. Early versions of the Panther were very unreliable and suffered numerous breakdowns. This situation was improved in later versions of the tank. The Panther had an excellent long 75mm gun, which could penetrate Allied tanks at ranges in excess of 1,000 metres. Its frontal armour could withstand all but point-blank fire from the Allied short 75mm gun mounted on the Sherman, but its much thinner side armour could be penetrated at long range. In later versions this situation was addressed, to some degree, by adding armoured side skirts and thickening the side armour. The curved gun mantlet could deflect a lucky shot down onto the thin armour above the driving compartment, which was easily penetrated, and this happened on at least one occasion to one of Kampfgruppe Peiper's Panthers.

Each panzer regiment had two battalions, one of which was equipped with Panthers. Owing to a shortage of tanks Kampfgruppe Peiper had only one composite battalion of Panthers and Mk IVs. Two companies, 1 and 2, were equipped with Panthers.

The 740th Tank Battalion was the only uncommitted armoured battalion in the whole of the US 1st Army. Unfortunately, its tanks had been withdrawn on 17 December, pending the arrival of new ones at an ordnance depot 4 miles north of Aywaille. All that was available to equip Captain Berry's C Company were fourteen Shermans, four Sherman DDs – amphibious tanks used on D-Day – and one M-36 Tank Destroyer. With this motley mix of armour, Berry set off towards Halte to try to block the German advance. In the meantime Lieutenant Macht's retreating column had reached Stoumont station, and found a 90mm anti-aircraft gun emplaced there. Captain Franklin Ferriss reported:

> As the withdrawing column passed Stoumont station, a 90mm AA gun was observed in position there. Its crew stuck by their gun and demolished at least one Mark VI [actually a Panther] tank and one half-track before their gun itself was destroyed. This slowed the enemy for a short time.

Oberscharführer Rudi Rayer, commanding 11 Company, also reports this action:

> The lead vehicle was destroyed by an anti-tank gun next to the railway station. At that point, I received orders to take the station in a dismounted attack. After overcoming slight resistance, the station fell into our hands.

By the time the Germans had taken the station and cleared the road, the Americans had been able to set up a strong defensive position. Lieutenant Colonel Robert Herlong's 1st Battalion of the 119th IR had arrived in the nick of time. His three rifle companies had formed a defensive line, with Macht's tanks, about half-way between Stoumont station and Halte. The terrain was ideal. The road ran close to the Ambleve River, and to the north the ground was heavily wooded and climbed steeply from the road. The enemy tanks had very limited ground to deploy onto and, although their infantry had no restriction on their deployment, they would be slowed by the steep wooded hill. The Germans' first tentative approach was seen off by Macht's tanks. Having been informed that Berry's company was on the way to replace them, Macht had no hesitation in firing off his last few rounds before he withdrew.

There then came a pause of about an hour, during which time Captain Berry's C Company, 740th Tank Battalion, got into position. Herlong then decided to make a combined tank-infantry attack along the road, as Captain Franklin Ferriss reported:

> At about 16:00 hours, the attack got under way. The tanks advanced in single file with their protecting infantry deployed abreast of them on each side of the road. Lieutenant Charles D. Powers' platoon was leading, with Lieutenant Powers' own tank at the head of the column. There was considerable ground haze in the valley, and Lieutenant Powers moved cautiously, realizing that all might depend on his spotting the enemy first. He hugged the inside of the road as he rounded a curve just west of Stoumont station. As he did so, the first enemy tank loomed into view, a Mark V, approximately 200 yards away, though barely discernible in the haze. Lieutenant Powers got off the first shot. It

Furthest point. As the three lead Panthers came around the corner in the middle of the photograph, towards where the photographer is standing, they were knocked out by Shermans of C Company, 740th TB. The stone tablet on the right marks the spot.

Furthest point. Shermans of Captain Berry's company waited on the road ahead for the arrival of Kampfgruppe Peiper, and halted their advance. The road to the left goes to Zabompre Farm.

ricocheted off the mantle of the Panther tank, and penetrated into the thinner armour just below, setting the tank ablaze. Lieutenant Powers advanced 50 yards, spotted another Mark V tank, and again got off the first round, which this time penetrated the lower front slope plate. The Mark V was disabled, though it did not burn. Lieutenant Powers moved on again and in another 50 yards, took another Mark V into his sights. This time his gun jammed. The Panther got off several rounds, which missed their mark and gave Staff Sergeant Charlie W. Loopey, commanding an M-36 TD behind Lieutenant Powers, the necessary few seconds in which to get off a round that pierced the Mark V's cupola, followed by several others, which caused the tank to burn.

The three knocked-out Panthers created a roadblock, and Herlong decided to move his infantry just beyond them and dig in for the night. Rudi Rayer also reported the final phase of the kampfgruppe's advance:

In the meantime, the rest of the battalion, after clearing the knocked-out tank off the road, continued the attack past the station mounted on the tanks. I was ordered to mount up the company and follow the battalion. After about one and half to two kilometres, the company ran into heavy enemy resistance. The 11. Kompanie was assigned to eliminate the dug-in enemy tanks and anti-tank guns in close combat by moving through the woods to the right of the road. It didn't work out and we were barely able to disengage from the enemy with heavy casualties. Then the company was used along with the rest of the battalion to provide cover to the right of the road in the woods. Shortly after, there was an enemy counterattack, which we repulsed.

Kampfgruppe Peiper had reached its furthest point. Critically short of fuel before he began his attack on Stoumont, Peiper had sent Gustav Knittel and his battalion back to Stavelot to try and open the route through the town again. He had also dispatched several columns north from La Gleize to try and locate enemy fuel dumps, but with no success, as each one clashed with enemy roadblocks and was forced to retreat. Peiper had no choice but to adopt a defensive position until fuel resupply reached him, and with this in mind he pulled his men back into defensive positions in Stoumont and La Gleize.

In Stavelot the 1st Battalion of the 117th IR had continued to push towards the river, with A and B Companies leading. By 12:00 hrs the whole of the town north of the Ambleve had been cleared of the enemy, with the exception of a few houses on the western edge, either side of the Trois Ponts road. South of the river the elements of the kampfgruppe which had not yet crossed gathered for another attack on the bridge, the north end of which was now back in American hands. The remaining Mk IVs of 6 and 7 Companies had been refuelled and began to advance on the bridge, along both the approach roads. One of the columns was led by several jeeps driven by men in American uniforms. Lieutenant Colonel Frankland knew that American troops had been engaged south of the river on the previous day, and seeing the jeeps caused him to pause. Deciding on safety first he called for artillery support. Captain Franklin Ferriss reported the effects of the defensive fire, and the subsequent German effort to cross the bridge:

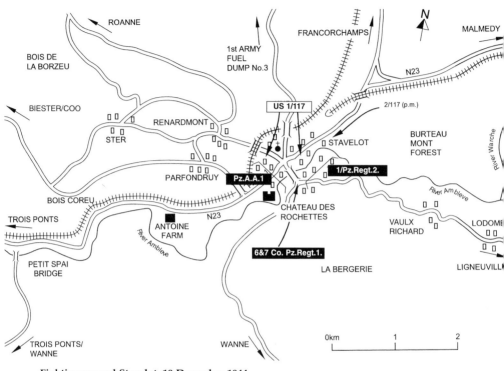

Fighting around Stavelot, 19 December 1944.

The town square in Stavelot. Fighting took place in and around the square as the advanced elements of the kampfgruppe pushed on towards Trois Ponts.

This had the effect of forcing the hostile infantry to deploy, and the tanks to string out. Most of the infantry became pinned down by American artillery and mortar fire. Those that did advance were stopped by small arms fire well short of the river. But hostile armour continued to roll forward. In particular, the column approaching Stavelot from the south-west managed to conceal itself behind the row of houses that lined this road, as it approached the bridge.

The last house on the road, short of the bridge, was about 40 yards from the intersection of the road with the other road that comes in from the south-east. In order to cross the bridge, enemy armour coming from the south-west was forced to expose its flank for this distance of 40 yards before being able to turn and advance frontally onto the bridge. One of Lieutenant McInnis's TDs (Sergeant Clyde Gentry, gun commander, and Corporal Buell Sheridan, gunner) had fortunately moved into an excellent position, with turret defiladed, to cover the bridge and the immediate approaches to it from the south.

Lieutenant McInnis and Sergeant Gentry had observed the enemy column moving into positions behind the row of houses south of the river. The gun crew waited expectantly. Suddenly a Mark VI tank nosed out from the protection of the houses and attempted to reach the turn, where its heavy frontal armour would protect it from 3-inch TD fire. Corporal Sheridan caught it, however, in his sights, and at a range of 125 yards, knocked its turret completely off with his second round. A few minutes later, a second Mark VI tried its luck. It managed to get to the intersection and started to advance across the bridge in the face of a hail of 3-inch fire. Before it had reached the half-way mark, a round apparently knocked out both its turret and its gun, for it was thereafter unable to traverse. Then two Mark VI tanks moved out. Ten rounds from Sergeant Gentry's gun stopped both of them. One had its track hit and got into a ditch in an effort to maneuver into a less vulnerable position. The other retired behind the protection of the last house, where it parked with its muzzle sticking out.

With this the German attacks from south of the bridge petered out. The Mk VI Tigers reported as attacking in the American accounts may have actually been refuelled Mk IVs from 6 and 7 Companies. One of 7 Company's tank commanders, Unterscharführer Roman Clotten, took part in the attack:

On the morning of the 19th December we were committed to an attack against Stavelot from Wanne, together with the remaining panzers from 6th Company (Obersturmführer Sternebeck), and were supported by a company of fallschirmjager. Advancing on the road from Wanne we found the eastern portion of Stavelot to be free from enemy forces. The portion of the town on the far side of the river was heavily occupied by the enemy and we were immediately fired on by anti-tank guns, mortars and infantry weapons. In spite of several attempts, the crossing over the bridge proved to be impossible.

During the morning of the 19th, Sturmbannführer Gustav Knittel had moved his battalion back to Stavelot, with orders from Divisional HQ to open the route back to the bridge. Knittel recounted his battalion's activities during the afternoon and evening:

At 1300 hrs the committed reconnaissance element reported that it discovered movement on the western edge of Stavelot. I initially committed the reinforced 2nd Company, Obersturmführer Coblenz, dismounted on both sides of the road and railroad line with the mission of attacking through to the Ambleve bridge south-east of Stavelot in order to establish contact there with Obersturmbannführer Sandig's 2nd Panzergrenadier Regiment, as the division had ordered. During the initial combat phase, the right flank of Coblenz's 2nd Company immediately suffered several killed and wounded. Shortly thereafter, an enemy battery opened fire against the attacking company from an unobstructed firing position on the hill north of Stavelot. It was clear to me that the 2nd Company could only accomplish its mission if the enemy battery could be eliminated from its dominant height. I had Obersturmführer Goltz's Headquarters Company in reserve, along with a reconnaissance platoon and an engineer platoon. I ordered Obersturmführer Goltz to commit the engineer platoon to eliminate the enemy battery and I myself set the reconnaissance platoon up to reconnoitre the Ster area in order to secure the northern flank of the 2nd Company attack. The 2nd Company attack stalled in the reinforced artillery and mortar fire from numerous batteries – I estimated 15. Any movement was impossible. Only after darkness did I learn from a 2nd Company messenger that it held approximately 12 houses on the western edge. In order to replace the company's heavy losses, I ordered the straggler elements of Headquarters Company's engineer platoon to assemble with 2nd Company and then be committed in the security line by Obersturmführer Coblenz. Simultaneously with the battalion attack from the west against Stavelot, the division ordered an attack by mixed divisional elements from the south-east, but enjoyed only limited initial success.

American accounts of Knittel's attack are very much in agreement with his account. Attacked by three panzers and about a hundred infantry, A Company of the 1/117th were driven back several hundred yards, until a heavy artillery concentration broke up the German attack.

Late in the afternoon the 2nd Battalion of the 117th IR moved into Stavelot to reinforce its sister battalion. The 118th Field Artillery Battalion continued to bombard the German forces on the south bank of the river, particularly those moving down the road towards the town. During the day it was decided to blow the bridge, which would greatly hinder German operations. There is some confusion about the actual date on which the bridge at Stavelot was demolished. One German account states that the bridge was blown on the 18th, although this can be discounted as there is clear evidence to show that the Germans tried to attack over the bridge on the 19th. Captain Franklin Ferriss's account had the bridge being blown on the 20th, but two other American accounts, by Lieutenant Colonel Dave Pergrin and Lieutenant Leland Coffer, state quite clearly that the incident took place after dark on the 19th. Coffer was the officer tasked with blowing the bridge, and his account of events has been followed.

Coffer was a platoon leader in A Company, 105th Engineer Battalion,

Members of the 1st Battalion, 117th IR, in house-to-house fighting to recapture Stavelot on 19 December 1944. *(Airborne Forces Museum)*

which was part of the 30th Division. At about noon on the 19th he was ordered to move to Stavelot and blow the bridge. First he had to reconnoitre the bridge and gauge how much explosive would be needed to blow it. Keeping under cover in the houses on the north bank, he managed to get a good view of the bridge without exposing himself to German fire. While there he also witnessed the engagement between the American TDs and the German tanks. Coffer decided that 1,000 pounds of TNT would do the job, and returned to his company command post to collect the explosives and his men. It was decided that the job would be done after dark, and under the cover of a mixed smoke- and high-explosive-artillery barrage. The smoke would give them cover from enemy observation, and the high explosive rounds would cover the noise of their movements. Coffer and his men approached the bridge carrying twenty 50-pound boxes of TNT. Coffer takes up the story:

> *Staff Sergeant James McKeon and Sergeant Lowell Richardson accompanied me with the rest of the men following, to set all the TNT in one stack directly over the thinnest part of the deck in the first span. The men delivered their boxes and quickly returned to the trucks. This was done in about 3 or 4 minutes and we*

three, McKeon, Richardson and myself, on a signal pulled all three fuse lighters simultaneously.

We took off running, disregarding any noise we might make, then a couple of short blocks away, 'KA-BOOM!!!'. It was a terrific explosion. Stone masonry houses close to the ends of the bridge collapsed and any remaining windows near the bridge were blown out. It must have been some shock to any Krauts, exposed or not, on the south side.

Coffer and his men had done their job well, and the northern span of the bridge had been demolished. Coffer's company commander, Captain James Rice, told a reporter, 'No German tank can broad-jump that.' He was right, no more German troops would cross the bridge at Stavelot.

By the close of the 19th the situation had become somewhat confused, so it is worth summing up the positions of the various elements of both armies. The main body of Kampfgruppe Peiper lay at Stoumont, La Gleize and Cheneux. Opposing them at Stoumont was the 119th IR of 30th Division, while elements of the 3rd Armoured Division were approaching La Gleize from the north. The 504th Parachute Infantry Regiment, 82nd Airborne Division, had pushed across the Lienne and occupied Rahier, south-west of Cheneux. At Stavelot the 1st and 2nd Battalions of the 117th IR had a firm grip on the town, and the bridge had been blown. To the west, Schnellgruppe Knittel was trying to push into the town and clear a route through to the bridge, while Rudi Sandig's kampfgruppe, based around the remaining two battalions of Panzergrenadier Regiment 2, had closed up with elements of Kampfgruppe Peiper on the south bank of the Ambleve. As midnight approached, the forces of both sides prepared to carry on the fight, in all areas, on 20 December.

The bridge over the Ambleve at Stavelot. After much fighting for its possession, the bridge was blown by Lieutenant Coffer during the night of 19 December 1944.

Chapter Seven

20 DECEMBER 1944:
PEIPER CUT OFF

During the night of 19/20 December the 3rd Battalion, 119th IR reorganized and formed a roadblock on the road leading north out of Stoumont. The battalion had suffered badly during the German attack on the 19th, losing 8 killed, 30 wounded and 203 missing. Of the missing, ten returned to duty on the 20th and 143 were released when the Americans recovered Stoumont and La Gleize. The battalion commander, Lieutenant Colonel Fitzgerald, had been relieved by Colonel Sutherland, the regimental commander. His place had been taken by Captain Carlton Stewart, assistant executive officer. Stewart worked wonders in restoring the battered battalion and resupplying them with heavy weapons, food and ammunition. The battalion manned its roadblock for over thirty-six hours, but their brittle morale was not put to the test, as Peiper did not send any of his men to the north along the road. By this time the kampfgruppe had no fuel to spare for carrying out such manoeuvres.

During 20 December the 30th Division received a welcome reinforcement when CCB (Combat Command B) of 3rd Armoured Division was attached to them. CCB's commander, Brigadier General Truman Boudinot, divided his command into three task forces – Task Force (TF) Jordan, McGeorge and Lovelady – all of which were involved in the continuing action against Kampfgruppe Peiper. Due to poor communications in the area, and the large frontage that the 30th Division had to defend, the troops in the area of Stoumont and La Gleize came under the direct command of Brigadier General William K. Harrison, 30th Division's Assistant Divisional Commander.

By the morning of the 20th, Peiper's forces were divided between three villages. In Stoumont, Peiper's main body defended the western end of the enclave against the 1st Battalion, 119th IR and Captain Berry's C Company, 740th Tank Battalion, the team that had brought the kampfgruppe to an abrupt halt near Stoumont station. To the north of Stoumont the survivors of the 3rd Battalion, 119th IR, blocked the road, and one of CCB's task forces, TF Jordan, was moving up behind 3/119 to carry out an attack on Stoumont. Peiper had left a substantial garrison in La Gleize to cover his rear and the road back to Trois Ponts and Stavelot. All roads to the north of the village were blocked by small American roadblocks, and TF McGeorge, CCB, and Company K of the 3rd Battalion, 117th IR, were approaching. Peiper's remaining element held Cheneux, to the south of the Ambleve, where the 504th PIR, 82nd Airborne Division was beginning to close in. The kampfgruppe was not in a very good situation. They were short of fuel, and,

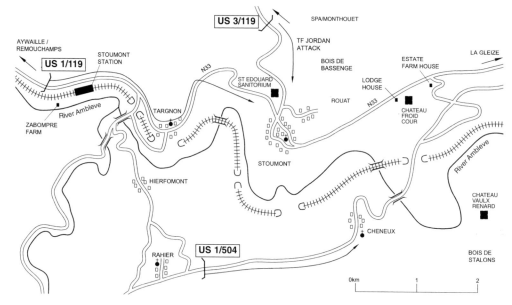

American attacks on Stoumont and Cheneux, 20 December 1944.

with the exception of the Stavelot road, were surrounded by American forces. Schnellgruppe Knittel and Kampfgruppe Sandig were still attempting to clear a route through Stavelot to enable supplies and reinforcements to reach Peiper. Knittel continued to attack the town from the west, while Sandig's men were still trying to force a crossing of the Ambleve, although their task had now been made doubly difficult by the blowing of the bridge, after dark on the 19th. All areas would see heavy combat on the following day, and, for the sake of clarity, each will be looked at in turn.

From the west of Stoumont, 1st Battalion, 119th IR, supported by C Company of the 740th Tank Battalion, continued their advance on the morning of the 20th. The commanding officer of the 740th, Lieutenant Colonel Rubel, described the advance:

> Our plan for the 20th was to attack at daybreak, seize Targnon quickly and continue rapidly to seize the town of Stoumont. The tank part of the job was to spearhead the attack and as soon as the village of Targnon was captured, to place two or more tank platoons on its high ground to support the attack on Stoumont. We asked the divisional artillery to fire on Targnon 'on call' only. They were also to fire several short preparations on Stoumont during the course of the previous night and to keep interdiction fire covering the road from Stoumont to La Gleize. The attack jumped off on the morning of 20th as planned and Targnon was taken by noon. Lieutenant Tompkin's (then Staff Sergeant) tank hit a minefield about 1,000 yards east of Targnon which blew

both tracks off. One enemy half-track, one Panther and one enemy held Sherman were engaged and destroyed during the day. The attack proceeded slowly from Targnon and by dark had failed to reach Stoumont by about 500 yards. Stoumont, like Targnon was situated on top of a hill and afforded perfect field of fire for the enemy. During the afternoon the enemy launched three heavy, fanatical counterattacks which drove our infantry back several hundred yards, but each time they were driven back, they quickly regained the ground.

Soon after starting out, the attack ran into the first opposition, a Panther tank. The lead American tank knocked the Panther out with its first shot, which 'opened its muzzle up like a rose'. Continuing towards Stoumont, the Americans knocked out two German half-tracks, but after this the main obstacle to the American advance was five small minefields, covered by German infantry. Company C, 740th TB, lost its first tank on a minefield, Staff Sergeant Tompkin's, just to the east of Targnon. By nightfall the advance had covered two miles and was only a few hundred yards from the western edge of Stoumont. It was at this point the fighting began to escalate, as Captain Franklin Ferriss reported:

There the leading tank, commanded by Lieutenant David Oglensky, was hit by a well-camouflaged direct-fire weapon, emplaced at the crossroads on the north side of town. The tank's gun was disabled, but the motor was alright. As it was almost dark, and too late to attack the town, Capt. Berry ordered Lieutenant Oglensky to turn his tank sideways across the road to form a roadblock. Lieutenant Oglensky did so.

To the north of the road was a large building, a sanatorium for sick children and old people, and this now became the focus of the fighting. Several platoons from B and C Companies of the 1/119th attacked the building, which dominated the western approaches to Stoumont, and after heavy fighting drove the German defenders out. Unterscharführer Karl Wortmann was a witness to this fighting:

We saw American tanks approaching, while heavy artillery was advancing along another road. These placed the sanatorium under very heavy fire. A large number of handicapped children, several old nuns and priests sought shelter in the cellar. Almost any enemy movement was visible to the naked eye. The Americans continued to approach, the firing became heavier. With its massive construction, the sanatorium looked like quite a fortress. However, the walls were being eaten away by the shells from enemy tanks, anti-tank guns and artillery. At the end, it looked like a ruin, the roof threatened to cave in. The few panzer men who were still not wounded did not want to give up. They continued the fight bitterly. It was clear to each man: The sanatorium had become a defensive bulwark. If given up, the Americans would have it easier in their approach to La Gleize. The Americans assaulted the sanatorium's ground floor. The panzer men withdrew to the upper floors. Bitter fighting, man against man, occurred. Our comrades threw hand grenades down the stairs to the lower floors and fired their rifles and pistols in order to open the way for a breakout from the fortress.

As hard as the German defenders fought, they were eventually driven out. Once the building had been taken the Americans found that they had another problem – 200 of the inmates had taken shelter in the cellar. Owing to the continuing fighting, any attempt to evacuate them would have to be postponed until the following day.

At approximately 23:00 hrs Peiper's men counterattacked the sanatorium. The building was so tactically important that the Germans had little choice but attempt to retake it. Jochen Peiper described the attack:

> *Against overwhelming American infantry strength attacking with tank support, Sievers, with three men left, was forced back into a room in the sanatorium. With panzerfaust and hand grenades, he fought his way from room to room clearing out the Americans who had gotten in, and with his pistol held off the infantry in the cellar. After a tank had been called up and swept the second floor clear with its cannon and machine gun, he was first to push into the cellar and destroy the enemy in close combat. The Americans repeated their attack twice, and each time they managed to push into the sanatorium because of their numerical superiority. It is only thanks to Obersturmführer Sievers' fanatical will to resist, coupled with his outstanding leadership ability and superhuman courage, that the sanatorium remained in our hands. This also guaranteed freedom of movement for the entire Panzergruppe, which had already been compressed into a narrow area.*

Obersturmführer Sievers left his own short account of the action:

> *The sanatorium was only given up for half a night and, in the counterattack, we took 40-50 prisoners and destroyed three tanks. The prisoners were taken to La Gleize. Stoumont was held until we were ordered to withdraw.*

Both German and American accounts talk of savage fighting that lasted for some time. The Americans were finally driven from the building, and B and C Companies, 1/119th, formed a new defensive line along a hedgerow about thirty yards to the west of the sanatorium. One small group, commanded by Sergeant William Widener, held on to one of the sanatorium's outbuildings. Captain Berry's tanks attempted to support the men of B and C Companies, but were caught by German panzers, as Captain Franklin Ferriss reported:

> *Three of Capt. Berry's tanks attempted without success to counter the hostile tank fire from positions along the road, just south of the sanatorium. They were greatly handicapped by the terrain, which sloped steeply up from the road to the sanatorium, while the enemy tanks were on even higher ground north of the sanatorium. Ascent up this slope was impossible due to the very muddy conditions of the ground, and the tanks were left on the road. Then Jerry had the bright idea of sending up flares to spot our tank's location. They were well-placed flares, which lit up the American tanks, but did not disclose the location of the enemy's armour. Two of Capt. Berry's tanks were knocked out in rapid succession. Thereafter all of the tanks were kept west of a house, approximately 150 yards short of the sanatorium, in order that they might be defiladed.*

With the withdrawal of the American tanks and infantry, the fighting at

The 3rd Battalion, 119th IR, and TF Jordan approached Stoumont along the N606, seen here.

Stoumont ceased for the day, although American artillery would continue to pound the German defenders throughout the night.

Earlier in the day the first of CCB's task forces carried out an attack on Stoumont from the north. TF Jordan, with Captain William Jordan commanding, comprised of two tank companies from the 33rd Armoured Battalion, and one company from the 36th Armoured Infantry Battalion. The task force advanced through the lines of 3rd Battalion 119th IR, and continued down the narrow road towards Stoumont, approaching to within 500 yards of the town before they were engaged by the defenders. Captain Franklin Ferriss takes up the story:

> There at a sharp bend in the road, the task force had two tanks knocked out by direct fire. The bend in the road enabled the enemy to fire the first shot, and the terrain was so steep and heavily wooded, that the tanks could not deploy off the road.

With the loss of his two leading tanks, and his inability to deploy the remainder of his task force, Jordan ordered his men to pull back. Peiper's men had held the town, but to their rear the sounds of fighting could be heard from the direction of La Gleize.

During the morning, Peiper had received welcome reinforcements. Hauptsturmführer Schelle's II/Pz.Gren.Regt. 2 had been dispatched by Rudi Sandig with orders to cross the bridge at Petit Spai and proceed to La Gleize.

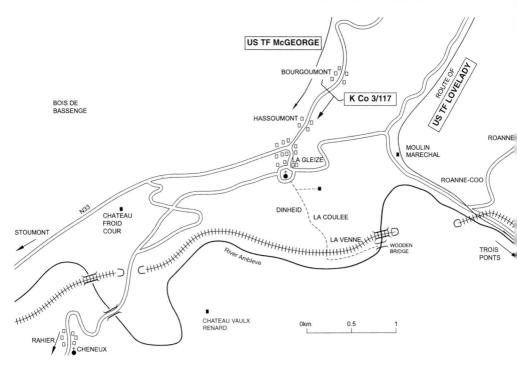

American attacks on La Gleize, 20 December 1944.

The Petit Spai bridge was not large enough to take vehicles, so the battalion had arrived at La Gleize on foot. Peiper deployed Schelle's battalion along the eastern edge of the village, in preparation for the highly probable American attacks.

The defenders' first sight of American movements was a column of tanks and half-tracks moving along the road to the east of La Gleize, in a southerly direction towards Trois Ponts. Several Tigers were deployed on the eastern edge of the village, but had too little fuel to allow them to deploy to engage the Americans. The enemy column, TF Lovelady, continued to the south and disappeared from sight.

Two separate American attacks took place along the road running north from La Gleize to Borgoumont. TF McGeorge, CCB, pushed towards La Gleize, but ran into heavy fire from Panthers of Panzer Regiment 1, and its lead tanks were knocked out. Major K.T. McGeorge, the task force's commander, then ordered his men to withdraw. The second American attack was carried out by Company K, 3rd Battalion, 117th IR, and its results are summed up by Captain Ferriss:

> *That same day, 20 December, Company K of the 117th Infantry was given the mission of capturing La Gleize from the north. It had reached the town of Cour*

the previous day, following its mission of blocking the enemy's exit northward from La Gleize. From Cour, it moved south to Borgoumont, but below Borgoumont it ran into very stiff tank and infantry opposition. The enemy's firepower was so great that it left no doubt that he was able to hold a very substantial garrison in La Gleize, even though his main strike force had gone on to Stoumont.

Had Schelle's battalion not arrived during the morning, the two American attacks may have had completely different results.

During the night of 20/21 December the Americans reorganized their forces around the Stoumont-La Gleize pocket. Brigadier General Harrison now had control of a number of task forces: west of Stoumont was Colonel Sutherland's 1/119th, with Captain Berry's attached tank company. To the north of the village was TF Jordan and 3/119th. These should have been fighting as a combined unit under the command of Lieutenant Colonel Courtney Brown, the executive officer of the 119th IR, but due to Brown remaining several miles from the battlefield at Halte, and the poor

A view of Cheneux sketched in April 1945. This is the direction from which the 1st Battalion, 504th PIR, attacked the village, suffering heavy casualties. *(Airborne Forces Museum)*

Stoumont

A view of the area crossed by the 1st Battalion, 504th PIR, as it attacked Cheneux.

communications in the area, both seem to have operated independently. K Company of the 3/117th came under command of TF McGeorge. Control of TF Lovelady, which had ended the day close to Trois Ponts, was transferred to the 117th IR.

While the 119th IR and CCB began to exert pressure on Stoumont and La Gleize, the 504th PIR made its move on Cheneux. The 1st and 2nd Battalions of the 504th were dug in at Rahier by first light on the 20th, while the 3rd Battalion had dug in at Froidville. In Cheneux the depleted 11 Company, Pz.Gren.Rgt 2, had dug into defensive positions, after returning from the fighting at Stoumont station on the previous afternoon. In support were the flak wagons of 84 Flak Abteilung. As has already been mentioned, II/Pz.Gren.Rgt 2 had arrived at La Gleize during the morning, and its 6 Company had been dispatched to Cheneux to reinforce the defenders. The German defenders were also in range to be supported by artillery positioned at Vaulx Renard, to the east of Cheneux.

At 13:00 hrs Lieutenant Colonel William E. Harrison, commanding 1/504th, ordered his B and C Companies to advance on Cheneux, while A Company moved to occupy Brume. Corporal Graves of Regimental Headquarters, 504th, saw the troops advancing towards Cheneux:

> At about 13:00 hours the 1st Battalion passed by the house on the road going toward Cheneux. The boys were in very high spirits and I heard one man shout out 'Four more shopping days to Christmas, pass it back.'

B Company led the advance, and made their first contact about 500m along the road to Rahier, with a German machine-gun team. Having killed one

Chateau
Froid Cour

La Gleize

Members of the 82nd Airborne Division in action near Cheneux. *(Airborne forces Museum)*

panzergrenadier and captured a second, B Company continued until they approached the western outskirts of Cheneux, where they ran into a wall of fire from the German machine guns and flak wagons. The diary of the 1/504th gives details of the attack:

> With 3rd Platoon on the left of the road and 2nd Platoon on the right, the Company continued the advance handicapped by ground haze which limited visibility to 200/300 yards and heavy machine-gun fire from the outskirts of the town. 1st Platoon was ordered by Captain Helgeson to turn the enemy's right flank. The captured enemy half-track was put between the attacking platoons, thus enabling the return of fire against the machine guns and 20mms. After receiving heavy fire, however, the half-track moved back. 1st Platoon advanced 200 yards past the other platoons' base of fire where it was pinned down by a 20mm and two MG42s with a squad of riflemen 100 yards from the enemy forward lines. Contact was lost with Battalion, and C Company's mortars were falling on the rear of the Company. The position then held by B Company was a tabletop criss-crossed by barbed wire fences. Ground haze made the adjustment of artillery difficult. At 1700 hours Captain Helgeson ordered the Company to withdraw 200 yards to the edge of the woods. An orderly withdrawal was made, one platoon at a time and the Company reorganized and set up a perimeter defence at the wood's edge. At 1845 hours Captain Helgeson gave the CO the situation.

Colonel Reuben Tucker, commanding 504th PIR, ordered Lieutenant Colonel Harrison to carry out a night attack on the village. B and C Companies would once again lead the attack, supported by two M-36 tank destroyers, and the attack would be preceded by a ten-minute artillery barrage. The attack commenced at 19:30 hrs, but the M-36s did not advance and the artillery barrage did not take place, so once again the paratroopers advanced into the teeth of the machine-gun and flakwagon fire unsupported. By 22:00 hrs the paratroopers had only advanced 400 yards, and Harrison had committed his HQ Company machine-gun platoon. One of the M-36s finally came forward and knocked out a 20mm gun that was holding up the advance. The attack ceased at 23:00 hrs, with the Germans still holding the main part of the village, while the Americans held the high ground on the western outskirts. The 1/504th had suffered 225 casualties, and its B Company was down to eighteen men, while C Company was only slightly stronger. At 23:00 hrs Colonel Tucker came forward to Harrison's command post. Harrison told him he could not advance without reinforcements, and Tucker promised him a company from the 3rd Battalion. These reinforcements would not arrive for several hours, and the next attack would not take place until the next day.

At Stavelot Rudi Sandig and Gustav Knittel were still trying to force a way through the town. Sandig had only his 1st Battalion left – his 2nd Battalion had crossed the Ambleve at Petit Spai and marched to La Gleize to reinforce Peiper, while his 3rd SPW Battalion had been attached to Kampfgruppe Peiper from the start of the operation. There seems to be some confusion between American and German sources as to exactly what part Kampfgruppe

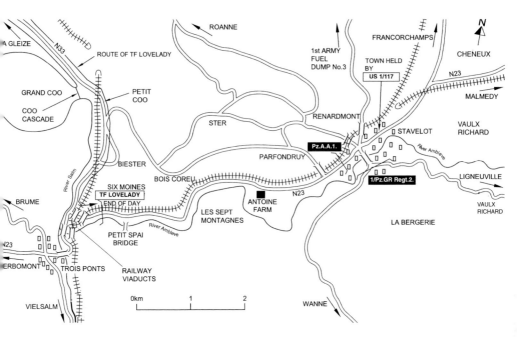

Fighting around Stavelot, 20 December 1944.

Sandig took in the events of 20 December. Captain Franklin Ferriss reported:

About 04:00 hrs on 20 December, two companies of German infantry made another effort to recapture Stavelot, this time by wading across the Amblève River (a distance of some 100 feet), and assaulting the town frontally. The swift current and the bitter coldness of the water made this a very difficult operation to coordinate. As a result, the fire-fight had started before most of the attackers had reached the north bank or even gotten into the water. To enable the 1st Platoon of Company A, which held the first row of buildings north of the river, to spot the German waders, flares were sent up and Lieutenant Hansen's tanks set fire to the houses on the south side of the river. Silhouetted against this light, the wading Germans made easy targets. At least half of the attacking force is believed to have been killed in the water, or forced back to the south bank. However, the hostile infantry was supported by direct fire, and this finally forced the First Platoon leader, Lieutenant Robert O. Murray, and his men to retire to the houses immediately behind the first row of houses. As soon as the Germans occupied the first line of buildings, however, the hostile tank fire was masked. Lieutenant Murray's men, with help from Company B on the left, launched a counterattack which drove the remnants of the attacking force back into the river. Only a small fraction of the original force succeeded in reaching the south bank. The American line was completely re-established along the

A sketch of Stavelot made in April 1945. After the heavy fighting of 18–22 December, the damage to the bridge and its surrounds is readily apparent. The view is from the south side of the bridge, the direction from which the Germans attacked. *(Airborne Forces Museum)*

north side of the river by 07:30. The lack of any enemy artillery supporting this counterattack was an important factor in its successful repulse.

On the other hand, Obersturmbannführer Rudi Sandig's report states:

The deployment was discovered by the enemy west of the Ambleve and he unleashed an unbelievable defensive fire. Light and heavy artillery, mortars, heavy machine guns, sharpshooters and later even low level attack aircraft dropped bombs on the entire surrounding area and fired on-board weapons at the battalion. There were very heavy losses! Further advance was impossible. Men sought cover in the basements to the right of the road. The distance to the blown bridge was approx 300m. Communications between the companies and to the battalion command post were impossible. Only limited messenger traffic was possible during the following night. Every movement was immediately covered by artillery and mortar salvoes. Particularly unpleasant were the enemy sharpshooters, who were well hidden in the houses west of the Ambleve.

This massive defensive fire lasted all day long. Only with the fall of darkness could the battalion commander, Sturmbannführer Richter, obtain an approximate picture of the situation his battalion was in.

These two accounts do not contradict one another but a problem arises with Untersturmführer Friedrich Pfeifer's account. Pfeifer commanded 2 Company of Richter's 1st Battalion, and was among the Germans who managed to reach the houses on the north bank of the river. Pfeifer wrote:

We maintained our position on the other river bank for about 18 hours but only had one MG left and no more ammunition. We had no contact anymore with the other bank. When dawn came [21 December] we began our retreat across the Ambleve, downstream from the bridge under heavy fire. I recollect the undertaking cost 23 men their lives. If the 4th Company had been on the spot and we had had reasonable fire support it might have looked different, but he (Sandig) had been too impatient.

Pfeifer states quite categorically that his men remained on the north side of the river until dawn on the 21st, whereas the American account says they were driven back by 07:30 on the 20th. Whatever the details of Sandig's attack on the 20th, during the night he ordered the 1st Battalion to withdraw and set up a defensive line 700–800 metres east of the Ambleve bridge.

By this time the Americans had heavy concentrations of artillery available to support them, and any build-up of enemy troops was mercilessly bombarded. The 1st Panzer Regiment's surgeon, Dr Sickel, set up his aid station within the chateau at Wanne, in the hills south of the Ambleve, and was on the receiving end of American artillery fire:

We set up our first-aid station in Schloss Wanne. It was a chateau with a relatively large interior courtyard and thick walls. For my first 'official duty' I placed the administrator and his staff under my personal protection, since they were threatened by civilians who wanted to plunder the seed. The stores in the cellars had already been partially removed. However, there were still sufficient supplies of provisions available. The American artillery soon had us spotted and shelled the castle with all calibres so that we could only load and transport our wounded behind splinter shields. Once a shell hit the kitchen wall directly above the ground level. The wall was shoved a quarter of a metre into the kitchen. The artillery rumbled day and night. We scarcely heard it any more. Allegedly, the American artillery fire was directed by a civilian from the church steeple. Wanne was actually a mixture of troop and main first-aid station. The transport of wounded was difficult because the roads were a total morass due to the thaw and, in some places, only tracked vehicles could move. Therefore, we were forced not only to bandage but to operate.

Throughout the area the Americans kept up a continual bombardment of the enemy positions, sometimes slow and steady, and at other times rapid and heavy.

Late in the morning Gustav Knittel ordered his 2 Company, supported by two King Tigers, to attack the west of the town. This time A Company,

An American 90mm anti-aircraft gun near Stavelot. Although intended for use against aircraft it was also a potent anti-tank weapon. One such gun was deployed in the centre of Stoumont during the kampfgruppe's attack on 19 December 1944. *(Airborne forces Museum)*

1/117th, was prepared for them. During the night a minefield had been laid between A Company's position and the enemy. Supported by tank and tank-destroyer fire, and having artillery support on call, A Company was able to stop the enemy, although it was a close-run thing. Part of the German infantry penetrated between A Company's 3rd Platoon, manning the roadblock, and the Company command post, in a large house 150 yards to the south. The Company Headquarters held its ground and brought the Germans to a halt, even though the Tigers were concentrating their fire on the house the command post was in. To their north 3rd Platoon was also having problems, as Coblenz's panzer grenadiers closed on their position:

> The attack got so close to the 3rd Platoons' positions, that Lieutenant Theodore V. Foote called for artillery fire only 50 yards away from his OP [observation post]. Before firing the concentration called for, the artillery liaison checked back with Lieutenant Foote. 'Yes, I know that it will fall where I am', the platoon leader replied, 'but that is what I want'. He got away with it, for none of his platoon was injured by the artillery fire.

The German attack finally became bogged down when one of the King Tigers was immobilized by having a track blown off.

During the afternoon, Knittel's men made another attack, this time 500 yards north of the road, in an attempt to outflank the American positions. The German infantry, unsupported by armour or artillery, were spotted silhouetted against the sky as they crossed a ridgeline. They were met by 3rd Platoon, C Company, 1/117th, with heavy sustained fire, and called down heavy concentrations of artillery fire. Once again the Germans came so close to the American positions that the artillery had to be called down on top of 3rd Platoon, but they had dug deep positions, and suffered no casualties. The Germans, 150 to 200 strong, suffered heavy casualties before the remainder withdrew.

The Americans in Stavelot were not the only problem Knittel had to deal with on the 20th. It has already been mentioned that an American armoured column had been seen proceeding down the road towards Trois Ponts earlier in the day by the defenders of La Gleize. This was TF Lovelady, which had been ordered to move towards Trois Ponts, and then on to Stavelot. Knittel turned some of his men towards Trois Ponts to combat this new threat. He was now forced to fight a defensive battle to his rear with his troops supported by 75mm anti-tank guns and a King Tiger. In the swirling mists of the river valley the Germans allowed TF Lovelady to advance to close range before engaging the leading American tanks, destroying six Sherman within minutes. With their leading tanks burning and blocking the road, the Americans withdrew back towards Trois Ponts as the daylight of the 20th began to fade. One American source, Captain Eaton Roberts, of TF Lovelady, states that the task force lost only four Shermans, while destroying a Mk IV tank, two trucks, one towed 150mm artillery piece, two towed 75mm anti-tank guns, three half-tracks, and a Volkswagen jeep.

Later that day elements of the 3/117th and E Company, 2/120th IR, occupied villages to the north-west of Stavelot, thus preventing a flanking move by the Germans taking the town from behind. Knittel's afternoon attack had come close to achieving this, as 3rd Platoon, C Company, marked the flank of the 1/117th's line. If the attack had gone in several hundred yards further to north-west it would have met little opposition.

Throughout the 20th, Peiper's adjutant, Obersturmführer Hans Gruhle, had attempted to establish contact with Division to obtain supplies of fuel and ammunition. Radio communications were poor and when contact was established it was fleeting and garbled. In the meantime, I SS Panzer Corps had managed to secure an air supply drop for Peiper, and 6th Panzer Army had confirmed this for 22 December. Peiper would have to fight on for two more days, unsupported and unsupplied. The plight of his remaining forces in the pocket looked grim indeed.

Chapter Eight

21 DECEMBER 1944:
A SHORTENING OF LINES

The 21 December followed the pattern of the previous day, as far as the German and American troops in and around La Gleize and Stoumont were concerned. American attacks on the two villages were interspersed by heavy artillery fire. Brigadier General Harrison's plan for the day was to make a 'squeeze play' on Stoumont. The 1st Battalion, 119th IR, with Captain Berry's tank company from the 740th Tank Battalion and an attached company of M-10 tank destroyers, would continue the attack in the area of the sanatorium on the western side of Stoumont. Due to heavy infantry losses the 1st Battalion had been reinforced by F Company from the 2nd Battalion. The remaining two rifle companies of the 2nd Battalion would swing around the north of Stoumont and cut the main road between the two villages, while the 3rd Battalion, with TF Jordan under command, would attack from the north once again.

All three of the 119th IR's attacks were due to commence before first light.

American attacks on Stoumont and Cheneux, 21 December 1944.

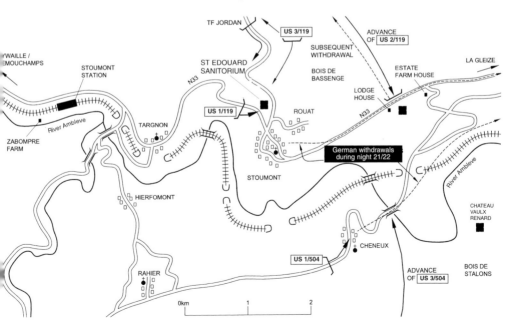

View of the Stoumont area.

The attack by 1st Battalion was delayed due to a counterattack by German infantry, as George Rubel reported:

> *The attack was resumed at 04:00 hrs. It moved forward about 100 yards when an AT gun knocked out the lead tank. Lieutenant Oglensky, who was riding the tank, found that his gun had been rendered useless and fearing that Jerry was about to begin a tank attack he placed his own tank crosswise in the road to form a roadblock. As he was doing this another shot hit his tank. He ordered his crew to get out and go to the rear, while he took over the tank immediately to the rear. He had hardly got aboard when an enemy panzerfaust hit the tank and the machine started to burn. He and his crew dismounted and almost at the same instant two more tanks were hit by panzerfausts. That left four tanks in the road – three of them on fire. The heat was so intense that it was impossible to get close enough to fasten a towing cable.*

The German counterattack commenced at about 05:00 hrs and continued for over two hours. The American attack on the sanatorium was put back until 12.45. While the Americans reorganized, Captain Berry's M-36, sheltered behind a house about 150 yards from the sanatorium, fired 240 rounds into the front of the building. This was later reinforced by several M-10 tank destroyers, which also fired two hundred rounds into the building. By the time the American infantry were ready to attack, the front of the sanatorium 'presented nothing but a series of gaping holes.' In the cellar were a number of wounded and civilians. One of these, Abbe Hanlet, left an account:

> *The American tanks fire point blank and incessantly into our walls which collapse over our heads. The grenades fall with a crash on the paving stones of the big hall and each time we were shaken. Somewhere near the kitchen a shell pierces the floor and brings down the cellar ceiling. Around the air vents of our underground hiding place bullets are raining and hit like hail stones during a storm. Every moment the house is shaken by shells. The crowd of 250 people regroup towards the centre around the nuns and away from the air vents. They pile on top of one another. One lies on the floor making oneself as small as possible; one would like to crawl into the ground so as not to be crushed by the house collapsing on our heads. One prays and begs with such fervour but it is impossible to say Mass and so instead one gives a general absolution. Suddenly, with dreadful noise, a shell has burst through the vault of our cellar, filling the dark underground room with smoke, acrid with dust and powder. People scream, howl and beg – 'Help! We're civilians!' In this tragic situation a priest rushes up the stairs to the kitchen to beg the fighters for a truce to evacuate the people but a German, seeing a figure in the darkness behind him, empties his revolver on the foolhardy messenger who, by a miracle, manages to get back to the cellar.*

Captain Berry's men had by some means acquired a 'Long Tom' 155mm self-propelled howitzer, and this was used in a direct-fire role against the sanatorium.

Infantry from the 1/119th attacked and gained a foothold in two rooms at the front of the sanatorium, before they became cut off. A Panther had moved up behind the building and was able to pin down the twenty-two surviving American infantrymen by firing directly through the ground floor. A bazooka team was dispatched to the roof of the sanatorium to engage the enemy tank but was quickly pinned down by machine-gun fire. It was left to Captain Berry and his tanks to save the day, as Captain Franklin Ferriss reported:

> *Capt. Berry's tanks came to the rescue. As previously stated, the tanks were unable to climb the slope from the road to the sanatorium, because of its steepness and boggy ground. But with the help of Headquarters Company of the 1st Battalion, Capt. Berry put in a 75-yard corduroy road, somewhat west of the sanatorium, which enabled the tanks to climb the hill to an elevation equivalent to that of the sanatorium. The three M-4 tanks and a TD [tank destroyer] gun then moved right up to the sanatorium. Lieutenant Powers, in the lead, managed to sneak around the right side of the 'chateau', and knock out the Panther tank, whose fire had been interdicting all movement in, to, or from the 'chateau'. The TD and the tanks then covered the withdrawal of the 22 infantrymen, who had been pinned down. After they had all gotten back safely, the American armour retired in the face of hostile AT fire from the high ground north-west of the sanatorium.*

More of Werner Poetschke's panzers were responsible for stopping the attack from the north of Stoumont by Task Force Jordan and 3/119th. To the east of the road the infantry of the 3/119th, supported by some of TF Jordan's light tanks pushed on to the edge of Rouat, where they held for some time. David Knox took part in this attack:

> *The artillery barrage started and we took off with it. No one showed any interest in going, but they knew it had to be done. It was so foggy that one of our men found himself ten yards from a German MG before he knew it. Collins was a hero here; he had knocked one position out with his Browning automatic rifle when it stuck. He grabbed the Jerry gun, turned it around and knocked the other crew out. It was too foggy, though; the attack just wasn't working. I told Captain Stewart that contact was lost on our right. There was nothing left to do but pull back. The first plan was to go back in again – immediately. Everyone had been pushed about as far as he could be. Nerves were being broken on men whom one would have thought would never weaken. Finally we got the word to hold up for the night. We organized with the light tanks and dug in.*

TF Jordan's M-4s were still restricted to attacking down the road and made little progress against the six German panzers defending this sector, getting no further forward than they had done on the previous day. Leaving an outpost watching the enemy, Jordan withdrew his tanks to Monthouet for the night.

As the 1st and 3rd Battalions of the 119th IR carried out their attacks from the north and west of Stoumont, Major Hal McCown led the remaining two companies of his 2nd Battalion, E and G, on a long foot march around the north of the village, receiving only sporadic mortar fire on the way. The battalion cut the road between Stoumont and La Gleize close to the Chateau Froid Cour, blocking the road with felled trees and mines. With the road blocked, McCown led some of his men towards La Gleize, but was captured in a short, sharp, fire fight with Georg Preuss's 10 Company panzergrenadiers. McCown would remain a 'guest' of Kampfgruppe Peiper for several days. With the other two prongs of his attack halted, Brigadier General Harrison decided that the 2nd Battalion's position was untenable, and ordered Major Nathaniel Laney, the battalion's Executive Officer, to pull his men back to the north of Stoumont.

The American 'squeeze play' had failed. Untersturmführer Rolf Reiser, Werner Poetschke's adjutant summed, up the day from the German perspective:

> *On 21st December the American attack again increased in intensity. As on the previous day they attacked into the sector north of the La Gleize – Stoumont road with tanks and infantry in order to block the road and break open our Stoumont defensive positions from the rear area. These attacks were repulsed by several Panthers from the 1st and 2nd Companies of the 1st Panzer Regiment and by grenadiers from the III.(gep.)/Pz.Gren.Rgt.2.*

While the Americans had attempted to take Stoumont, TF McGeorge continued its attack on La Gleize. During the morning the defenders of La

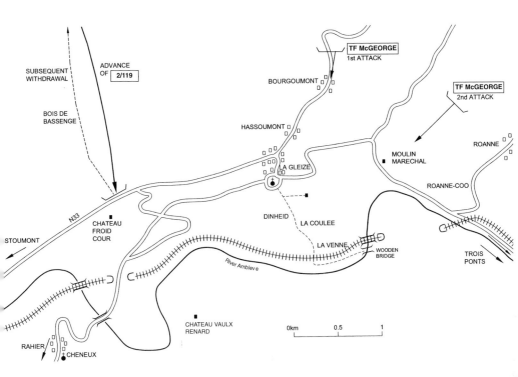

American attacks on La Gleize, 21 December 1944.

Gleize had received a small but welcome reinforcement, as Unterstumführer Hennecke reported:

It was on 18th December, during the attack against Stavelot our company commander, Obersturmführer Kremser, was wounded. My vehicle was also hit. I climbed into the company commander's panzer and ordered my driver, Rottenführer Bahnes, to take our panzer to the maintenance shop. Today, on 21st December, we were encircled at La Gleize and Stavelot was again in the hands of the Americans. We heard the sounds of armoured vehicles coming from Trois Ponts. We drove our panzers into position in order to give the attacking Americans a reception. Out of the morning fog appeared the first panzer. Thank God I recognized in time that it was a Panther. When number 111, my vehicle, was noticed, the 'open fire' order was rescinded. The turret hatch of the panzer opened and a shape left the vehicle with raised arms. A second followed – my driver, Rottenführer Bahnes! He described how, immediately after the end of the fighting in Stavelot he had begun to repair the panzer. He took parts from another shot-up panzer. When the Americans pushed back into Stavelot he did not leave, rather he kept still and quietly went on with his repairs. The Americans did not concern themselves with a wreck. During the second night someone knocked on the vehicle. A straggler, a Wehrmacht Oberleutnant, who had determined that the panzer was occupied and wanted to be let in. After the repairs, the wagon could run in 3rd and 4th gears, so he resolved to follow us with it. He taught the Oberleutnant how to operate the turret. Then they were off. With a fiercely turning turret the Panther raced through Stavelot. The Americans were so disconcerted that they were unable to bring any anti-tank gun into position in time to shoot at the panzer. Bahnes was promoted to Unterscharführer and awarded the Iron Cross for this 'stroke of genius'. Unfortunately, he was killed in the last days of the war.

Bahnes's actions show the determination of the Germans to reach their objectives!

TF McGeorge continued its attack along the road north of La Gleize. American Shermans were channelled along the road and ran into direct fire from a number of German panzers as they tried to negotiate a tight S bend. After losing two tanks McGeorge ordered the remainder to withdraw. His accompanying infantry made some progress, but were also forced to pull back. McGeorge then tried to outflank the German positions, early in the afternoon, but ran into Obersturmführer Handtusch's King Tiger and Hauptsturmführer Klingelhofer's Mk IV at Moulin Marechal, which forced the Americans to withdraw. Blocked on both approaches, McGeorge left behind a screening force, and swung to the east of the village, with the intention of attacking along the main Trois Ponts road from the south-east. Fortunately for McGeorge, the panzers defending the Moulin Marechal area had been withdrawn into the main defensive lines at La Gleize, and could not interfere with his manoeuvre.

Cheneux, looking back towards La Gleize. The Dinheid feature is the high ground on the right.

The Americans continued to pound La Gleize with artillery and mortar fire – over 100 guns – making any movement very dangerous, as Panther commander Eugen Zimmermann found to his cost:

On 21st December I was severely wounded by a mortar fragment in the right arm and hip in La Gleize while I was dismounted from my Panther. During a pause in the firing, I was carried by my comrades into the La Gleize church. I can still clearly see the red cross flag hanging from the church. At that time, the church was full of wounded and civilians so I had to be placed close to the church doors. This proximity to the exit was apparently my salvation. No sooner was I laid down when tanks and artillery fired at the church. A large stone fragment struck a severely wounded comrade next to me. I did not know him. I only knew he was thirsty! – 'I'm thirsty', he groaned – I was too, but there was nothing to drink. The firing on the church caused great panic, especially among the civilians. For me, there was only one thing to do: get out! I crawled to the exit. I was overrun by those capable of running, but I got out and was able to find cover between some gravestones. I made it to the graveyard steps where I recognized two US medics who were our prisoners the day before. The two of them carried me, almost passed out across the street into a basement.

The panzer crews had little comfort remaining within their tanks, as Heinz Hofmann of 1 Company recollected:

December 21 passed under heavy artillery fire, since the enemy had probably detected our mortars which had been set up in the farm across from us. We were inside the tank day and night. First of all, that gave us the best protection against the artillery fire and, second, we were an outpost, so we had to be ready to go at any minute. I still remember clearly that we used empty lemonade bottles for urinals, as we didn't want to expose ourselves to fire unnecessarily. We wrapped ourselves in blankets inside the tank, as it was fairly cold at that time.

On Peiper's southern flank the paratroopers of the 504th PIR continued their pressure on the defenders of Cheneux. Their 1st Battalion had received a bloody nose in its attack on the village on the 20th, and had been reinforced during the night by G Company of the 3rd Battalion. The Americans probed the German defences during the night, but were driven off. At 08:00, after half an hour's artillery preparation, the Germans counterattacked in an attempt to retake the high ground on the western edge of the village, but were in turn repulsed with heavy losses. Both sides had reached an impasse. Corporal Graves gave a vivid description of the area the American paratroopers had fought over on the previous day:

After walking about a mile up steep, heavily wooded hills we came to a road junction where five German vehicles had been knocked out. The surrounding area was the worst example of what happens when a great number of men are killed and wounded that I ever saw. Broken rifles, loose ammunition, countless helmets, bloody GI clothes and bandages, all sorts of miscellaneous equipment, belts of machine-gun ammo and mortar shells, were strewn around the bald

American bazooka team in position to oppose advancing German vehicles. The rear man is in the process of loading a rocket into the weapon. *(Airborne Forces Museum)*

hilltop and ditches alongside the road – not to mention the dead. The living, glassy eyed and expressionless, were hugging their holes scraped out of the banks bordering the road. The overall scene was so sickening that it made you want to shout out to God and ask him why all this was necessary.

During the morning and afternoon of the 21st the remainder of Lieutenant Colonel Julian Cook's 3rd Battalion advanced on, and captured, Monceau, a small village to the south of Cheneux. At nightfall both sides issued orders. The German defenders were to withdraw to the defensive perimeter at La Gleize, while the reinforced 1/504th would once again attack Cheneux, and Cook's H and I Companies would attack north-east from Monceau towards the Vaulx Renard bridge. The 82nd Airborne Division's commander gives a vivid account of the attack on Cheneux:

The fighting at Cheneux was increasing in bitterness. On this date [21st] the first battalion of the 504th, assisted by a company of the third battalion of that regiment, made a final, all-out assault on the Germans in that town, and in close hand-to-hand fighting, many of the parachute troops jumping aboard the German half-tracks and knifing the Germans at their posts, the Germans were driven back across the Ambleve River and our troops seized the bridge. In this attack we destroyed a considerable amount of armor and killed and captured many Germans from the 1st SS Panzer Division.

This is a highly dramatized account of the taking of Cheneux! By the time the Americans went in, the Germans had withdrawn to La Gleize, leaving only a very small rearguard. Due to lack of fuel, Peiper's men had to abandon most of their vehicles and heavy weapons. The 504th's report records that fourteen flak wagons, six half-tracks, four trucks, four 105mm howitzers and one King Tiger were found abandoned in the village. All the vehicles had empty fuel tanks, and the guns had run out of ammunition. While the 1/504th consolidated their position in Cheneux, the 3/504th continued to push up to the Ambleve, where after receiving fire from the Germans across the river, they dug in. On the morning of the 22nd the badly battered 1st Battalion was withdrawn into reserve. Corporal Graves, who had watched them advance to attack Cheneux, laughing and joking, saw them return:

The shattered remnants of the 1st Bn came straggling listlessly down the road, a terrible contrast to the happy battalion which had only two days before gone up the same road wisecracking and full of fight. They were bearded, red eyed, covered with mud from head to foot, and staring blank-facedly straight to the front. No one spoke.

The German defenders of Cheneux must have looked the same as they withdrew across the Ambleve into La Gleize.

By nightfall on the 21st Peiper was in a desperate situation. His men were spread over a large area holding a number of villages and outposts – Stoumont, Cheneux, La Gleize and Moulin Marechal. Division had informed him of an attempted relief by Kampfgruppe Hansen, the third kampfgruppe of the Leibstandarte. Hansen would push across the Ambleve and reinforce

Knittel, and the combined force would push through to La Gleize, probably on the 22nd. Desperately short of fuel, ammunition and men, Peiper decided to withdraw all his surviving men into a tight perimeter at La Gleize, and turn the village of scattered houses and farms into an all-round fortress, where he could await Hansen's arrival. The fuel situation had become so desperate that Division had attempted to float half empty jerrycans down the Ambleve to Peiper!

During the early evening the Germans began their withdrawals into La Gleize. Chateau Froid Cour, between Stoumont and La Gleize, was being used as an aid post. The Germans did not have the transport to move all their wounded comrades, and Untersturmführer Rolf Reiser recalls:

In the lower rooms of the palace lay more than 100 German wounded, most of whom had to be left behind. Only the lightly wounded and those capable of being moved were to be taken to La Gleize. It was difficult to bid farewell to those left behind, especially with an imploring look and a squeeze of the hand we had to make known our inability to help.

Only the lightly wounded, and the unwounded American prisoners, including Hal McCown, were taken back into La Gleize. It must have been heartbreaking for the SS men, many of whom had experience on the Russian Front, where the Russians systematically killed any SS men captured, to have to abandon their wounded. Fortunately, this was not the Russian Front and the Americans looked after the eighty remaining wounded Germans well when the chateau was captured on 22 December.

During the night of the 21st, the kampfgruppe received a message from Division giving both good and bad news. The good news was that an air resupply would be attempted on the following night. The bad news was that Hansen's attempted relief had been halted. Peiper was in a very tight spot, and his men were on their last legs. Unterscharführer Rolf Erhardt summed up the situation:

We had been hungry for days, many had nothing to eat at all. It was the same with sleep. We couldn't think about it. I believe that since the start of the attack I was able to get more than one hour of unbroken sleep only once or twice. In general, all of the comrades, whether simple soldiers or commander, had long surpassed the limits of their capabilities. Faces were unshaven and unwashed, eyes were red and we were all cold. Many had been wounded.

Without relief the kampfgruppe was doomed, and it is to this relief that we must now turn.

Kampfgruppe Hansen was the third kampfgruppe of the Leibstandarte, and was formed around the three panzergrenadier battalions of Max Hansen's Pz.Gr.Rgt.1. Hansen had advanced along a more southerly route than Peiper and Sandig, and had been ordered to turn north by the Divisional Commander, Oberführer Wilhelm Mohnke. Leaving his 2nd Battalion to cover his left flank along the Salm River, Hansen moved his two remaining battalions north to the area of Wanne and Aisomont. Elements of the American 505th PIR, part of the 82nd Airborne Division, had crossed the Salm

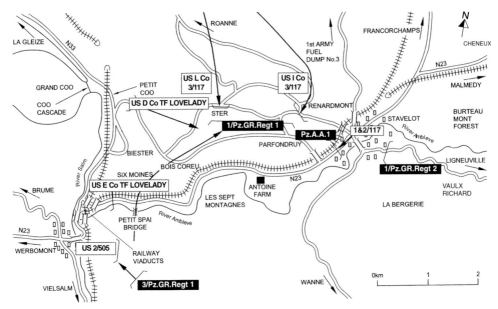

Fighting around Stavelot, 21 December 1944.

River and occupied the Wanne Heights, between Trois Ponts and Wanne. Hansen dispatched his 3rd Battalion, commanded by Hauptsturmführer Bottcher, and supported by a company of Jagdpanzer IVs, to drive the American force back across the Salm. Bottcher's men struck E Company of the 2/505th and put them under heavy pressure. F Company crossed the river to support E Company at 1330, but with pressure continuing to build, both companies were ordered to withdraw late in the afternoon. The withdrawal turned into a rout, and engineers were forced to blow the bridge in the face of the advancing Germans. American sources state that a company-sized force of Bottcher's men attempted to wade the river, but were repulsed.

Hansen ordered his 1st Battalion, with another company of Jagdpanzers, to cross the bridge at Petit Spai. They were then to join with the remnants of Schnellgruppe Knittel and force a way into Stavelot from the west, with the objective of clearing the town and the site of the demolished bridge. Heinz Krumpen, a member of one of Hansen's werfer batteries, was among the first troops to cross:

> *From Wanne we continued in the direction of Aisomont. Shortly after this town we drove past a children's home that lay on the right side of the road and then into the Ambleve valley. We crossed the Ambleve over a bridge that later collapsed under the weight of one of our own panzers. Then we crossed the Trois Ponts–Stavelot road and set up our werfers in positions on a forested hill to*

range Stavelot. We could support the attack of the I Battalion companies against Stavelot from these positions, in part with smoke shells.

As the panzergrenadiers of Hansen's 1st Battalion began to cross the bridge, the Divisional Commander, Oberführer Mohnke, decided to take a risk and ordered the Jagdpanzers to start crossing. Hauptsturmführer Karl Rettinger, commander of the Jagdpanzers, witnessed the results of Mohnke's decision:

In the Wanne area, the battalion received orders to advance to assist the Panzer Regiment extract itself from its situation. In order to bring relief, the Ambleve had to be crossed. However there was no crossing site available in the area that was suitable for panzers. There was only one single bridge that, in my opinion, was only suitable for trucks. However, the Divisional Commander wanted us to try anyway and ordered me to use the bridge (a hopeless attempt!). As anticipated, the attempt had to fail. The first assault gun, with the commander of the 1st Company, Obersturmführer Holst, broke through and fell into the river. The crew abandoned ship; only the driver remained in the panzer. After giving exact instructions, he was rescued. Then the engineers were brought up and a new bridge was to be built. After it was almost finished, high water came and carried it away!

Another witness to this episode was Gunther Junker of 3 Company, Pz.Gr.Rgt.1, who recalled:

Leaving the assault guns, we marched in combat formation to a farmhouse and were immediately hit by artillery. A small bridge crossed the Ambleve. Then three assault guns arrived. The first drove slowly onto the bridge and while on the bridge it tried to steer, which tore the bridge loose from its anchor and it fell into the river with the assault gun. Bridge in! Geschutze in! Man OK! We feverishly tried to make it to the other side, using ladders and what not. Most of us took a bath! On the other side of the river stood a shot-up enemy tank, but it had also caught one of ours. We climbed a hill. One of the other companies was engaged in heavy fighting in a town. Because of poor terrain we could not attack. We then occupied positions at the edge of a forest for the night.

Pioneers were rushed forward in an attempt to repair the bridge, but American artillery quickly put a stop to the work, as Unterscharführer Klaus Schonewolf reported:

Their forward observers monitored our bridge construction site, and the losses suffered by our engineers were devastating. The losses had to be replaced by non-engineers. Because of this and the constant harassing fire, the work progressed poorly.

Without the support of heavy weapons and Jagdpanzers, Hansen's men made little progress and stalled on the Renardmont-Ster line.

American plans in the Stavelot area were to clear the remainder of the German troops on the north bank of the Ambleve between Stavelot and Trois Ponts. While TF Lovelady's E Company group held firm near the railway viaduct at Trois Ponts, D Company, commanded by Lieutenant Richard Edmark, was to advance on Parfondruy. I and L Companies of 3/117th were

American gunners move a 57mm anti-tank gun through the mud. The 57mm M1 was the standard infantry anti-tank gun.

to advance from the area of Roanne on Renardmont and Ster respectively. Finally, 1/117th, supported by elements of the 743rd Tank Battalion, was to clear the western edge of Stavelot.

Edmark's company and I and L Companies made good progress throughout the morning, but were brought to a halt around Ster and Renardmont, when they collided with Hansen's 1st Battalion, advancing north from the river. Edmark was ordered to move towards Stavelot, but became engaged in a fire fight with tanks from the 743rd Tank Battalion. This friendly fire episode was almost certainly caused by Edmark's tanks advancing along the wrong road, and being mistaken for German panzers.

On the western edge of Stavelot, Manfred Coblenz's 2 Company of Schnellgruppe Knittel came under severe pressure throughout the day. Coblenz described his situation:

I was in the first house on the left side of the street. The Americans employed a reinforced combat patrol at this house. They were able to work to about 30 metres but because I had a better position I repulsed them after a heavy fire fight and with hand grenades. The enemy disengaged himself. The artillery fire continued with short interruptions until evening. The general situation was very critical.

A rottenführer in Coblenz's company recalled:

We, the 2./Pz.AA1, were located in about 12 to 15 houses on the extreme edge of Stavelot, west of the Stavelot railroad station. We had heavy fighting behind us and had suffered heavy losses. The company was very weak. On the afternoon of 21st December we faced a heavy American attack by tanks and infantry from the front and infantry through the wooded ravine in the left flank of the III Platoon. The attack against III Platoon was threatening the entire company. The enemy advanced approximately 50-60m, but was then thrown back. After the battle, Untersturmführer Siebert constructed a front to the west, for us, therefore, to the rear, because we anticipated the enemy from that direction. But the enemy then attacked at midnight with tanks and infantry from the north-west, but we were able to repulse him again.

By the end of the day Knittel's men had held their positions under severe pressure. Instead of taking Stavelot and relieving Peiper, with the help of Hansen's men, they were fighting for their own survival. One of Knittel's men summed up the situation:

On 21st December III Platoon had only a few men. These had not slept all day and had no more to eat, and they had to constantly stand guard. We were completely exhausted and at the end of our nerves! One man already had a nervous breakdown.

Peiper had withdrawn his men into a tight perimeter at La Gleize. The Americans were unaware of his withdrawal from Stoumont, where the three battalions of the 119th IR, Captain Berry's tank company and TF Jordan readied themselves for another assault on the town on the following day. To the north and east of La Gleize TF McGeorge prepared to attack again. Between Stavelot and Trois Ponts Schnellgruppe Knittel and Hansen's 1st Battalion were hemmed in by TF Lovelady and the 1st and 3rd Battalions of the 117th IR, with their supporting troops. The bridge at Petit Spai was down, but during the night German pioneers built a footbridge across the Ambleve, close to the fallen bridge. The climax of the operation was approaching.

Chapter Nine

22 DECEMBER 1944:
THE PRESSURE BUILDS

The Americans prepared to attack Stoumont once again. This time on the 22nd, with the 1st and 2nd Battalions, 119th IR, attacking from the west, and the regiment's 3rd Battalion, with TF Jordan, attacking from the north. The key to the defence of the western edge of Stoumont was the sanatorium, which had been attacked unsuccessfully on the previous two days. At about 10:00 hrs Brigadier General Harrison arrived at the 1st Battalion's position to try and 'figure out how to attack the place.' Captain Franklin Ferriss reported:

> He [Harrison] *noticed that nothing was drawing fire from the building, and then two civilians reported that the Germans had vacated it during the night. The General ordered a reconnaissance patrol to investigate. It found the place deserted, and the 1st Battalion had occupied it without firing a shot. Two or three seriously wounded Americans, whom the Germans had left behind in the sanatorium, reported that the enemy had vacated the building at 04:00 hours that morning.*

Members of the 504th PIR advance towards the front close to Cheneux on 22 December 1944. Note the 57mm anti-tank gun on the right of the photograph. *(Airborne Forces Museum)*

Men of the 82nd Airborne Division advance through thick woodland typical of the terrain through which much of the fighting took place. *(Airborne Forces Museum)*

There were still signs of enemy activity in the main part of Stoumont, but an attack from the west by the 1st and 2nd Battalions quickly cleared the remaining enemy presence from the village. The Americans pushed on and occupied the Chateau Froid Cour, where they found sixty badly wounded German soldiers. These were quickly evacuated.

The 1st Battalion had borne the brunt of the fighting at Stoumont and had lost 106 men. Of these, eighteen had been killed, sixty wounded, and twenty-eight were missing, although twenty-four of these were recovered when La Gleize fell. Surprisingly, not a single one of the 200 civilians sheltering in the cellar of the sanatorium was wounded, and they too were rapidly evacuated to safety.

Late in the day the 119th IR prepared itself to attack the western side of La Gleize the next day. The 2nd Battalion was left to defend Stoumont, while the 1st and 3rd Battalions moved forward into their jump-off positions for the following day. The 3rd Battalion, with TF Jordan, would advance along the N33, the main road between Stoumont and La Gleize, although the light tanks of TF Jordan would attack along a more northerly route. 1st Battalion, with Captain Berry's tank company, would advance on the more southerly road between Stoumont and La Gleize, which passed through La Gleize Station. Little if any contact seems to have been made between the Americans and the German troops defending the western edge of the town during the day.

Peiper's only aggressive move that day was to send a column of armour and infantry north from La Gleize towards Les Tscheous. The column was led by a captured Sherman. American artillery observers spotted this column and pounded it with artillery fire. The Sherman was quickly destroyed, followed by the other three tanks in the column: a King Tiger from 3 Company, and two Mk IVs from 6 Company. By 15:00 hrs the surviving infantry had withdrawn back into the main German positions.

The only serious attack on La Gleize came from TF McGeorge. Having been stopped in its tracks on the previous two days, McGeorge had moved his troops to the south to attack the town along a new axis from the east. After an intensive thirty-minute artillery barrage, McGeorge began his attack at 14:00 hrs. After losing two tanks to mines and a further two to tank fire, TF McGeorge withdrew to the line of the Roannay stream at about 15:15 hrs. This attack had been more successful than McGeorge could have realized, as one German defender, Unterscharführer Rolf Erhardt, described:

A large number of American Shermans appeared on the back slope road. The cannon of our Panzer IVs were useless due to the distance. The long 8.8cm cannon of the two Konigstigers and the Panther's 7.5 cannon had it easy with the Shermans since they could out-range them at this distance. The American formation was recognized early enough and we were able to take up suitable firing positions. After the first Tiger fired and missed, the Shermans formed from an unexpected front and began firing rapidly. This drove me in a hurry from my observation post on the first floor to the basement. We followed the fighting from there. The Americans shells blew through the houses; the

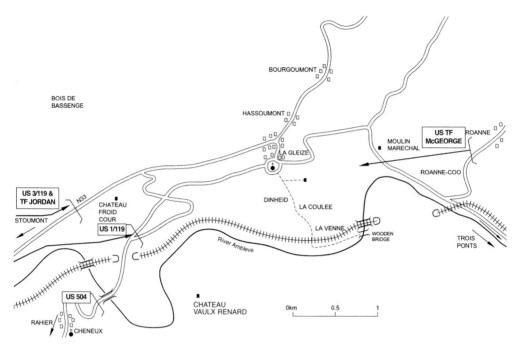

American movement around La Gleize, 22 December 1944.

basement was overfilled with people. Plaster and broken stone fell from the vaulted ceiling. The shots from our Tigers could easily be distinguished from the incoming shell bursts. In our own thoughts we decided that every shot by an 8.8 was a hit. Suddenly the Tiger commander, Untersturmführer Handtusch, plunged into the basement with both hands pressed against his head. His Tiger had taken several hits, which had shaken up his sensitive weapons system so much that the electric firing system had been put out of order. Another hit on the cupola wounded Untersturmführer Handtusch in the head and he had to abandon the smoking panzer, which could catch fire at any moment. Minutes later, the second Tiger commander, Obersturmführer Dollinger, arrived in the basement without a word; he was bleeding from the head. After he was bandaged he reported that smoke from the firing had made the observation of targets impossible. The rapid succession of enemy rounds had eliminated the last chance for a hit. The numerical superiority of approximately fifteen Shermans negated the weapons superiority of our panzers. Obersturmführer Dollinger's Tiger had also received a direct hit that amputated the forward third of the cannon. This made a state of depression noticeable, which had never been so openly recognizable. After these losses and the shortage of everything, what would the next day bring?

PzKfw VI Ausf. B 'King Tiger'

Panzerkampfwagen Mk VIB Königstiger (King Tiger).

Crew:	5
Weight:	69 tons
Speed:	23 mph
Main gun:	88mm KwK 43 L71
Machine guns:	3 x 7.92mm MG
Maximum armour:	180mm

The King Tiger first saw action in May 1944 on the Russian Front. It was a heavily armoured monster, and put dread into many Allied tank crewmen. Its armour made it slow once it moved off road, and its size made it difficult to hide, which made it prey to Allied fighter-bombers. It was also very unreliable, as was its predecessor the Tiger. Its gun was one of the best anti-tank weapons of the Second World War. With a muzzle velocity of 1,200 metres per second it could penetrate Allied tanks at very long range.

To make up for having only one battalion of tanks in Panzer Regiment 1, Kampfgruppe Peiper had the 501st Heavy Tank Battalion attached to it. With a paper strength of forty-five tanks this was a very powerful unit. Unfortunately, its commander, Sturmbannfuhrer Hein von Westernhagen, was only ever able to field a fraction of this number because of mechanical breakdowns. Most of the King Tigers lost by the kampfgruppe were abandoned after running out of fuel.

Although the Americans were unable to penetrate the Tigers' thick armour at anything but short range, damage to gunnery systems, or to the gun itself, rendered the Tigers useless, which greatly decreased the defensive capabilities of the troops in the Werimont Farm area. Dollinger's Tiger remains in La Gleize to this day.

TF McGeorge's attack was the only one of the day, but the defenders of La Gleize were not having a quiet time. By now the Americans had a large number of guns ranged in on the town, and observers on the heights above. American artillery fire was virtually non-stop. A number of the defenders have left their accounts of what it was like to be on the receiving end of the American shellfire:

Obersturmbannführer Jochen Peiper:

Our position in La Gleize had become very difficult. The town is surrounded by mountains and offers very excellent artillery observation points to the enemy. The forest is very close to the town and offers very good lines of approach for infantry. In view of the great enemy artillery superiority, it was only a matter of days before the whole town would be shot to rubble. It was hardly possible to move in the streets. All squares of the streets were under direct machine gun and tank destroyer fire.

Unterscharführer Karl Wortmann:

A large American gun was in position approximately 200m in front of us at the edge of a forest. We could make out the Americans with our naked eyes. Soon they were firing heavy phosphorus shells into the town. After the fourth round the church steeple crashed slowly to earth. The gun continued to fire and the rounds whistled over our heads at low altitude. We watched from our positions as the town – our wounded and the civilian population were in the basements, schools and churches – slowly sank into debris and ashes. It died that day, as did many of our comrades.

Rottenführer Heinz Hoffman:

The artillery fire increased enormously. Breaks in the firing occurred, but not in any way where you could determine when they would be. The civilians across from us left the houses to take cover in dugouts. Anyone who didn't absolutely have to be outside took cover from the artillery bombardment. Midday, towards 14:00 hrs, the bombardment increased tremendously. After two hours most of the houses in our part of the village were in ruins, especially the upper floors and gables. At the time the bombardment began, we, that is different men from both crews, were in the cellar of our farmhouse. At the time, Obersturmführer Preuss's command post was also in the cellar.

Finally, Untersturmführer Reiser:

After a half-quiet night the enemy had not attacked and we had long ago become used to constant artillery fire, a steadily increasing drumfire greeted the morning. Contact with leaders in the defensive positions was only possible by messenger. The messengers made indescribable efforts on that day, moving through murderous artillery fire within direct view of the enemy.

The Americans were slowly but surely pounding La Gleize and Peiper and his men into dust. The pressure on the German defenders was extreme. Peiper seems to have stood up well to the strain, as is evidenced in two accounts, one German and one American. Rottenführer Rolf Erhardt operated as a messenger, and was often in Peiper's command post:

There was a lot of activity in the command post. Runners and officers came and went almost continuously. The faces were not only marked with exhaustion, but were also very serious and hard. Obersturmbannführer Peiper was calmness itself. You hardly ever saw any sign of emotion. When he received a report of the death of an infantry officer who was close to him, I saw his face from close up. His mouth became tighter, insofar as that was still possible. His eyes became slits and he clenched his fists, as if he wanted to break something – but only for a second. Then the tension vanished, and he was as he always was. He asked technical questions and issued orders. He didn't swear and he didn't raise his voice. That was Peiper, who during this hopeless phase of the fighting at La Gleize, as during his entire career, gave even the least of his men a degree of support and security that few officers in the unit could.

The detritus of war. SS Panzergrenadiers look through the wreckage of an American column. *(Airborne Forces Museum)*

The other account comes from Hal McCown, who had a number of lengthy conversations with Peiper during his brief captivity, and who gave a description not only of Peiper, but also of his men:

> An amazing fact to me was the youth of the members of this organization – the bulk of the enlisted men were either eighteen or nineteen years of age, recently recruited but, from my observations, thoroughly trained. There was a good sprinkling of both privates and NCOs from years of Russian fighting. The officers for the most part were veterans but were also very young. Colonel Peiper was twenty-nine, his tank battalion commander [Poetschke] was thirty; his captains and lieutenants ran from nineteen to twenty-seven.
>
> Morale was high throughout the entire period I was with them, despite the extremely trying conditions. The discipline was very good. The noise discipline on the night movements was so perfect that I could hardly believe that they could accomplish it. The physical condition of all personnel was good, except for lack of proper food, which was more strongly apparent just before I escaped from the unit. The equipment was good and complete, with the exception of some reconditioned half-tracks among the motorized equipment. All men wore practically new boots and had adequate clothing. Some of them wore parts of American uniforms, mainly the knit cap, gloves, sweaters, overshoes and one or two overcoats. I saw no one, however, in American uniforms or in civilian clothes.
>
> The relationship between officers and men, particularly the commanding officer – Colonel Peiper – was closer and friendlier than I would have expected. On several occasions Colonel Peiper visited his wounded and many times I saw him give a slap of encouragement to heavily loaded men, and speak a couple of cheering words.

Of Peiper himself, McCown had the following to say:

> I have met few men who impressed me in as short a space of time as did this German officer. He was approximately 5 ft 8 inches in height, 140 lbs in weight, long dark hair combed straight back, straight well-shaped features, with remarkable facial resemblance to the actor Ray Milland. He was completely confident of Germany's ability to whip the Allies.

It is obvious from this description that both Peiper and his men made a great impression on the American officer.

Night fell over La Gleize, and the clouds cleared to leave a clear moonlit night. At 20:00 hrs the promised German air resupply arrived, in the form of three Junkers 52 transport planes. Karl Wortmann witnessed the drop, and took part in the attempt to recover the canisters:

> At approximately 20:00 hrs we heard heavy motors droning in the sky. We knew that no enemy aircraft were flying that evening; they were German Ju 52s. There was some moonlight that evening, giving the pilots the opportunity to search for a suitable location to drop the supply containers. The containers hung from parachutes and fell slowly to earth. We could see them clearly. We marked the locations where they had come to rest. With two groups of three men

each we went to fetch the containers. We clearly saw several land in an open meadow, but it was between us and the American positions. We approached to perhaps 30–40m, and then the enemy opened up with heavy machine-gun fire. We tried to crawl further. Don't even think of it! The last couple of metres were denied to us by a hail of fire. The enemy rounds whistled to the left and right of us. We were happy just to crawl back out of there without losing anyone. The whole night through we could not get those canisters out of our thoughts. On the following day we saw through binoculars that quite a number of the supply canisters were lying in no man's land, which was only 200m wide. A light snow was falling, but we could still easily make out the canisters and the parachutes. Our cursing did not help us any!

The inexperience of the German aircrews, and the limited size of the drop zone, resulted in 90 per cent of the promised supplies falling into American hands, or in No Man's Land.

To make matters worse, during the evening Peiper received a radio message from Division giving him very bad news, as Untersturmführer Rolf Reiser at Peiper's command post reported:

During the night a Division radio message informed us that the attack by Gruppe Hansen was suspended and, therefore, there was no longer any hope for relief. During the commanders' briefing (Peiper, Poetschke, Diefenthal) the question of a breakout from the La Gleize pocket was raised for the first time. On the basis of a sober assessment of the hopeless situation, Obersturmbannführer Peiper requested over the radio permission from Division to break out.

Fighting around Stavelot, 22 December 1944.

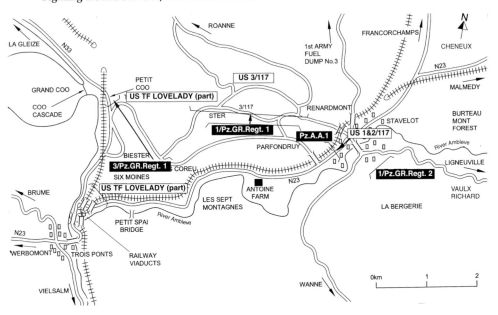

The attempt by Kampfgruppe Hansen had failed to break through, and it looked unlikely that any further progress would be made. All Peiper and his men could do was wait for permission to break out.

During the night of the 21st/22nd Hansen had been ordered to continue his drive towards La Gleize. With this in mind he moved two companies of Bottcher's 3rd Battalion across the river and assembled them at Coreu. Hansen's 1st Battalion would attack from its positions around Renardmont and Ster, while 3rd Battalion would attack towards Coo and then along the main road from Trois Ponts to La Gleize. The 1st Battalion got off to a bad start when its commanding officer was killed, as Gunther Junker, an eyewitness recounted:

In the early morning I observed that there were troop movements on the other side of the woods. My report to battalion received the reply: '1st Company is forming up for an attack!' When I then saw a machine gun being set up in position against us, I sent another report to the command post. Unfortunately, the hazy light would not allow us to determine whether it was friend or foe. The messenger returned with the battalion commander Sturmbannführer Karst, and another officer, to see for themselves. According to my report, the commander walked a little way into the wood and was immediately shot. A comrade, who tried to carry him back, was also killed. Another succeeded. My platoon then had to reconnoitre the edge of the wood, whereby I was wounded.

Karst was replaced by Hauptsturmführer Rink, but the I Battalion attack made little progress against the 3rd Battalion, 117th IR, and elements of TF Lovelady.

Hauptsturmführer Karl Bottcher's III Battalion made much better progress, and pushed through to Petit Coo. Oberscharführer Nebel, from 12 Company, took part in the attack:

I received orders from Hauptsturmführer George to reconnoitre the slope along the road leading to Petit Coo. After moving about 2km we reached a clearing and saw a gun in a farmhouse directed at the road. In spite of good camouflage, we were discovered and placed under fire by mortars. We withdrew to the departure positions. After Hauptsturmführer George returned from his command briefing, we received the decisive attack order. It was aimed at the relief of Panzergruppe Peiper, which was encircled in La Gleize. We marched, adjacent to the 11th Company on the left, through the forested hills and attacked Petit Coo. The eastern edge of the village was reached after suffering light losses. The battalion penetrated further into the town, while I was ordered to locate a command post in the town itself. I set out with Unterscharführer Stork and Sanitatsunterführer Erdelen. The men of 11th and 12th Companies took cover in the houses along the road. Several were burning. At one street corner I entered a building, it was a shop. Suddenly, a burst of machine-gun fire tore over my head into the shop. Stork and Erdelen climbed through a side window into the building. We rushed up the stairs and saw that a tank was standing next to the building across the street. Now, nothing but escape! We left by a basement window in the rear of the building and entered a garden, running into the first men of our battalion behind a hedge. After a pause to rest, I realized that my face and hands were completely covered with glass splinters. I was bleeding heavily.

On the receiving end of the German attack was Captain Eaton Roberts, a medical officer with TF Lovelady:

Early in the afternoon on the 22nd December, the present writer returned to Petit Coo from the command post and engaged in replacing a radio in his jeep. One of the light tankers noticed a group of soldiers walking towards us, in the distance. The radio was disregarded temporarily, its aerial left unconnected.

A German Nebelwerfer, known to the Allies as 'Moaning Minnies' due to the sound its projectiles made. A frightening and effective weapon.

Sturmbannführer Gustav Knittel (right), commander of 1st Panzer Reconnaissance Battalion, confers with his adjutant, Obersturmführer Leidreiter, during the fighting to recapture Stavelot.

Had it been in operation, a frantic warning from Major Stallings would have been heard, telling us to get out of there in a hurry.

Standing complacently in the doorway of the aid station, previously a restaurant, we watched, with little more than mild interest, the advancing soldiers, silhouetted against the sunlit hillside.

We recognized them as enemy troops when they were about 200 yards away. There were about fifty of them, but more came over the crest of the hill until approximately eighty were counted. They advanced in approved infantry fashion, irregularly dispersed and about six paces apart. Nonchalantly, and with no effort at concealment, they marched towards us, utterly disregarding our plainly visible tanks, whose guns were now threateningly trained upon them. With admirable presence of mind, seen so infrequently among tankers, the B Company men held their fire until the enemy was about 50 yards away.

By that time, our aid station personnel were so intrigued by the attack, in which no shots had yet been fired, and so confident that our light tanks could annihilate what we thought was simply a large patrol, that no effort was made to escape.

Finally, the tanks opened up smartly and in unison, with their .30-calibre bow guns, spraying the thoroughly exposed German infantry mercilessly.

Many fell, but many more continued their advance, still marching almost at attention, polished black boots and aluminium mess equipment shining brightly.

Then our tanks began firing their 37-millimeter guns loaded with high explosive ammunition among the foe. More fell, and more advanced, seeking cover behind the buildings on their side of the road.

Now the Germans began to fire rifle and other small arms at us, the first round shattering a large mirror behind the doorway we had been standing in. This brought us, the medical section, to the shocking realization that we were not watching a training film, and in fact, were in the midst of a fire fight. Judiciously, we repaired to the basement, there to discuss our sad predicament.

After a brief 'council' Roberts and his men made a break for it, across an open field into a slightly sunken railway line, and then on to Grand Coo. Unfortunately, only the first five men made it, the sixth man was shot and killed by an enemy machine gun, and the remaining two stayed in the cellar and were captured. The Germans knocked out two light tanks, and captured a number of prisoners, including the two medics, and the bulk of Lieutenant Grey's reconnaissance platoon.

Bottcher's men were unable to advance any further. Without heavy weapons, and under increasing artillery fire, they were unable to push on towards La Gleize. The III Battalion's commanding officer, Hauptsturmführer Bottcher, was wounded during the attack. Hansen had to call off the attack, and informed divisional headquarters, which passed the information on to Peiper at about 17:00 hrs.

Schnellgruppe Knittel, now reduced in strength to little more than a company, still desperately hung on to a number of houses on the western edge of Stavelot. Shortly after first light, 1st Battalion, 117th IR, began its attack to recapture the town. Progress was slow but steady. The German defenders were so determined to stand their ground that the Americans had to demolish the houses around them. By last light a handful of men remained holding the Chateau Lambert. Coblenz had been wounded and captured, along with Droge, the Pioneer Platoon leader. Gustav Knittel described the fighting that day:

> *The enemy shelled the advance defensive line of Company Coblenz and the attached engineer platoon with tanks until they were ripe for attack, and then broke into their positions with a surprise assault with tanks and an assault troop and forced the company to withdraw. This is how the last survivors of the engineer platoon, with their platoon leader Droge, Obersturmführer Coblenz and about 18 officers and men from the 2nd Company ended up in American captivity.*

By the end of the day both sides were exhausted. The German attack had been brought to a halt. Few reinforcements were available, while the Americans fed the 2nd Battalion, 120th IR into the line in support of TF Lovelady. Both sides had large numbers of guns and mortars deployed in the area, and continued to pound the enemy's positions throughout the night. Both American and German troops on the front line hunkered down in their foxholes, sheltering from the enemy barrage, and awaited what the morrow would bring.

Chapter Ten

23 DECEMBER 1944:
THE END IS NIGH

The attacks by the 1st and 3rd Battalions of the 119th IR both began at 08:30 hrs on 23 December. The 3rd Battalion was to advance along the N33, the main Stoumont-La Gleize road. The first obstacle the battalion encountered was the roadblock established by G Company, 2nd Battalion, two days before, which had been improved by the Germans, and was covered by tank and automatic weapon fire. One of TF Jordan's tanks was knocked out as it approached the roadblock, and it took until 13:10 hrs to clear the way. The battalion then advanced another 150 yards before it was held up by 20mm and anti-tank fire from enemy troops stationed in La Gleize.

L Company, 3/119, advanced through the woods to the north of the N33, and Lieutenant David Knox took part in the attack:

American attacks on La Gleize, 23 December 1944.

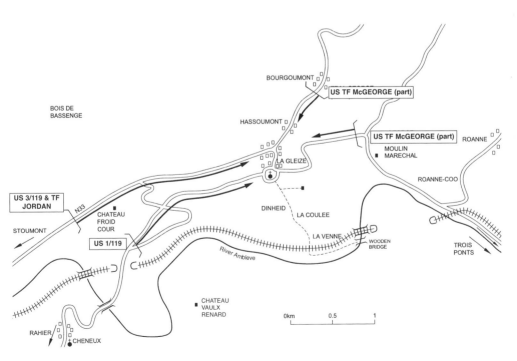

The next morning we took off for La Gleize. It had been a very cold night. Frost was on the ground. The three rifle companies were to approach the town over three different roads or routes. According to the map it looked good – phase lines to check in on and all sorts of big plans. We started on the way. By noon we realized that we were on about the only road there was and also that the road we were on didn't seem to be on the map. It was very confusing. There was no route into the town. Over on the other side of the next draw we could see a red parachute that had been used to drop supplies to the German troops. There was supposed to be an air show that afternoon, but something happened and it didn't come off. This was the first good day since the breakthrough. The planes were probably used on more important objectives [The American aircraft had dropped their bombs on Malmedy, many miles to the east by mistake, killing and wounding a number of American soldiers and civilians]. *Night came and we ground-hogged for the night. The order came down that all troops would have gas masks by midnight. The Germans must really be making this thing 'all out'. That whole night was spent in trying to get artillery lifted that was falling very near our third platoon. Everything was being dropped in La Gleize that night. Everything. As I shivered I thought, 'Tomorrow is Christmas Eve'.*

The one thing that the 3rd Battalion attack had achieved was a link with elements of TF McGeorge, close to the Nabonruy stream at 13:20 hrs. The line around Kampfgruppe Peiper was complete.

The 1st Battalion's attack made a little more progress, reaching the La Venne crossroads before it met any resistance. One Sherman was disabled in a minefield laid by the Germans to cover the crossroads, while a second was knocked out by anti-tank fire. The minefield was cleared, and the battalion advanced a further 300 yards before it was halted by flanking fire from a Panther and a Mark IV positioned on the Dinheid feature, to the south of La Gleize. The 1st Battalion was supported by two self-propelled tank destroyers from A Company, 823rd TD Battalion. The company commander, Captain Bruce Crissinger, was asked by Colonel Herlong, 1st Battalion's commander, to see if he could do anything about the enemy tanks. Crissinger and Lieutenant Cunningham set off on a foot reconnaissance. On the way they spoke to an infantry soldier who said he was an 'OP'. As an artilleryman Crissinger understood 'OP' to mean observation post, but the infantryman meant outpost, and Crissinger and Cunningham continued into No Man's Land between the opposing forces. A burst of machine-gun fire forced the two American officers into a ditch. After a while Cunningham took his chance and headed back towards friendly lines, while Crissinger kept his head down. Crissinger takes up the story:

In about half an hour I heard footsteps on the road. Someone kicked me on the foot; I turned over and there were two German soldiers looking at me. One carried a sub machine gun and the other a rifle. They wore either tanker or paratrooper helmets. They took everything I had of value, broke the M1 I was carrying and we took off down a bank to the right of the road to a railroad track,

La Gleize. The village was held for several days by the kampfgruppe, and reduced to rubble by American artillery fire.

picked up some tank ammunition that had been dropped by plane and then climbed a steep bank to a grove of evergreens.

Crissinger was escorted back into La Gleize, where he met Hal McCown.

While the two battalions of the 119th IR made little progress on the western side of La Gleize, TF McGeorge was putting in another attack from the east. McGeorge planned a two-pronged attack to commence at 09:00 hrs. The more northerly prong comprised K Company, 3/117, D Company, 36th Armoured Infantry, and 2nd Platoon of A Company, 743rd Tank Battalion. It would attack from the area of Borgoumont towards Les Tscheous. The Sherman tanks of McGeorge's I Company would supply the second prong, and would attack up the N33. The infantry attack made some progress and captured Les Tscheous, but was counterattacked by German panzers, which recaptured part of the village. McGeorge dispatched a section of Shermans from I Company, but these were held at bay by flanking fire from German tanks at Hassoumont. The American infantry, although under heavy pressure, managed to hold its ground. The remainder of I Company advanced along the N33 and reached the area of the Werimont Farm, but were also halted by flanking fire from Les Montis and Hassoumont.

All things considered, the Americans had made little progress against Peiper's positions around La Gleize during the attacks throughout the 23rd. Peiper had realized that his men could not hold out for much longer against continuing American pressure and the incessant artillery bombardment. The

SS Panzergrenadiers pass burning American vehicles. These are members of Kampfgruppe Hansen, which attempted to relieve Peiper at La Gleize during 22/23 December 1944.

(Airborne Forces Museum)

morale of the kampfgruppe had begun to weaken, as a radio operator from Pz.Rgt 1 recalled:

At La Gleize, morale was very muted, almost fatalistic. Naturally, we didn't let our heads hang. But there, for the first and only time in combat, I had the feeling that I wasn't going to get out. From the military radio station in Calais I had heard that the Leibstandarte had been surrounded at La Gleize and was awaiting annihilation there. Airborne supply wasn't working. As a result, there was almost no fuel or ammunition left. Morale was down to zero.

Peiper made a renewed request for permission to break out of the pocket. Division passed the request to 1st SS Panzer Corps, who then passed it on to 6th Panzer Army, who denied permission. Priess, commander of 1st SS Panzer Corps, left the decision to Wilhelm Mohnke, who, being aware of the true situation, gave Peiper permission. It has been stated that permission was granted on condition that Peiper would bring out all his wounded and vehicles, but this is ludicrous. Peiper had no fuel left to move his remaining vehicles, and without motor transport could not contemplate moving his seriously wounded men. Peiper's only option was to break out on foot. Peiper sums up his tribulations while he awaited permission:

'Last chance for breakout this evening without wounded or vehicles. Please approve.' Convinced I would receive permission to break out during the course of the day, I immediately began to make the necessary preparations and put together a plan. While my radio officer was busy trying to re-establish radio contact, he continuously asked 'Where is the main line of resistance? Where is the artillery support? May we break out?' During the afternoon, our preparations for breaking out had advanced to a point where there was no turning back.

Untersturmführer Rolf Reiser was at Kampfgruppe headquarters when permission was received for the breakout:

At 14:00 hrs the division issued the order by radio to break out of the La Gleize pocket. Obersturmbannführer Peiper discussed possible breakout routes on the map with his commanders. The enemy situation and the course of the main combat line was unclear. The main problem was the crossing of the Ambleve in the south of La Gleize unnoticed by the enemy. The leader of a kommando from 'Unternehmen Greif', a naval Oberleutnant that had fought his way to us at La Gleize, was ordered to cross the Ambleve and reconnoitre enemy security in that sector. At twilight, the Oberleutnant and two of his men broke out to conduct this reconnaissance which was important for us. Meanwhile, the order to prepare for the breakout was issued and the company and unit commanders were summoned to the command post for the last orders issue. The men from 'Unternehmen Greif' had, in the meantime, returned and reported that the railroad viaduct and the old wooden bridge across the Ambleve were questionable for the breakout. There were American security forces located in a railroad crossing guard's house between the railroad viaduct and the tunnel located to the east. They were posted there to guard the bridge. These guards had to be eliminated by a surprise raid so that the Ambleve crossing and the main combat line could be reached. The men from 'Unternehmen Greif' were ordered to eliminate the American bridge security. After this mission was accomplished by the 'Greif Group' raid, the men in the panzer group – there were still some 800 men – would cross the wooden bridge unnoticed by the enemy and make their way to the main combat line.

Peiper and his staff worked tirelessly on all the details necessary for evacuating the remaining 800 soldiers of the kampfgruppe from the La Gleize pocket without alerting the Americans to what was happening. Peiper knew he couldn't take his most seriously wounded along with him, and these would have to stay behind in La Gleize. Diefenthal's medical officer, Obersturmführer Dr Willibald Ditmann, and Unterscharführer Rolf Fricke, of Poetschke's headquarters company, volunteered to stay behind to look after the wounded. Further volunteers were requested to stay behind to man the defences to give the impression that the kampfgruppe was still fighting, and also to destroy the panzers and vehicles that would have to be abandoned owing to empty fuel tanks, after Peiper's men had withdrawn. Peiper also discussed with Major McCown and Captain Crissinger the question of the responsibility for the American prisoners sheltering in the cellars of La Gleize. McCown sums up these discussions:

He [Peiper] told me he had received orders from the commanding general to give up his position and withdraw to the east, to the nearest German troops. He knew it to be impossible to save any of his vehicles, that it would have to be a foot withdrawal. His immediate concern was what to do with the American prisoners, of whom he had nearly 150 as well as his own wounded. He dictated to me a plan of exchange whereby he would leave all American prisoners under the command of the senior PW [prisoner of war], a captain, to be turned over to the American commander as the Americans entered the town the next day. He said his wounded would also be left in the cellars of La Gleize and he would leave a German medical officer in charge of them. He had previously left a considerable number of wounded in the chateau at Stoumont. In exchange for the American prisoners, all German wounded would be turned over to the 1st SS Panzer Division, wherever they might be when the wounded were assembled. I would then be released back to the American lines, as I would be the only prisoner retained during the foot movement of the Germans east from La Gleize.

The American captain mentioned by McCown was Crissinger. McCown made it clear to Peiper that he could not guarantee that the exchange would be made as requested as the decision had to be made by higher headquarters.

During this period Unterscharführer Rolf Erhardt recalled:

During the last days of the action in La Gleize, I was in this basement as a messenger. It felt like a dovecote, messengers constantly coming and going. All of the faces not only reflected the strain, but also proved to be serious and hard. Obersturmbannführer Peiper was the embodiment of calm. He hardly ever showed any emotion. He asked his questions and issued his orders in a businesslike manner. There was no expression of feeling, no cursing, no loud words. That was Peiper, who had given so much support and security to the last of his men at this time.

Peiper gathered his senior officers together during the evening for a final briefing. Rolf Erhardt goes on:

The last orders were issued in La Gleize during the evening of 23 December. I cannot remember the names of all present. Besides Obersturmbannführer Peiper, were Hauptsturmführer Diefenthal, Sturmbannführer Poetschke and other officers. A map was laid out on a heavy stone table. All the officers presented their views. Then the order to break out was issued: 'Along the Basse-Bodeux road through Trois Ponts to the south.' The meeting ended with the establishment of the time and the password: 24th December – 02:00 hrs – password 'Merry Christmas'.

Peiper sent a final radio message to divisional headquarters at Wanne: 'I'm heading south-east through the woods with smoking socks!'

While Peiper prepared to break out during the night, Hansen was ordered to make yet another attempt to break through to La Gleize and relieve him. These plans came to nothing, as General Leland Hobbs, commanding 30th Division, prepared his own operation to clear the Germans from the north bank of the Ambleve. Hobbs had placed the 2nd Battalion of the 120th IR under command of the 117th IR. Its E Company had in turn been attached to TF Lovelady, where, in conjunction with the light tanks of Lovelady's B Company, they were to attack along the N33 and retake Petit Coo from the

Fighting around Stavelot, 23 December 1944.

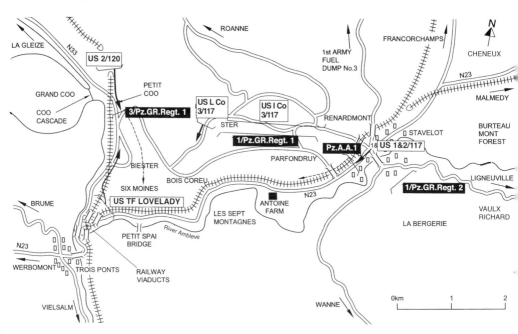

Stavelot after the battle. To the left of the bridge is one of the kampfgruppe's King Tigers, which had been damaged and abandoned during the fighting.

north. From the area of Trois Ponts Major Stalling's battle group would attack Petit Coo from the south. Stalling had been cut off by the advance of Bottcher's battalion, but had more than held his own. L Company, 3/117th, would attack Point de Vue de Ster, while I Company would hold Ster and Renardmont. Finally, the 1/117th would push along the N23 from Stavelot towards Trois Ponts.

Bottcher's 3rd Battalion, now under the command of Obersturmführer Haft, held the villages of Petit Coo and Biester, and prepared to advance, but were struck by the advancing tanks and infantry of TF Lovelady. In heavy fighting the battalion's 12 Company was almost annihilated, but one of the few survivors, Oberscharführer Nebel, described the action:

> During the night the Americans pulled out of the town and placed it under fire the next morning. Obersturmführer Hasse's command post was located with the Panzerschreck [bazooka] Platoon in a building on the edge of Petit Coo. An enemy tank was set up at the entrance to a tunnel. Our Panzerschreck Platoon was to put it out of action and lost all of its weapons. Today I do not personally know those who were killed, because a large portion of the men had arrived just before the operation. Obersturmführer Hasse was killed during the further course of the fighting. Our battalion commander, Hauptsturmführer Bottcher was also seriously wounded in this fighting. Obersturmführer Haft from 10th Company took command of the battalion.

The American advance was slow but steady. Petit Coo was taken at 11:15 hrs, but Biester did not fall until 16:00. The 3rd Battalion had lost the bulk of its 12

A view over Stavelot drawn in April 1945. The view is from the high ground to the north of the town looking south towards the Ambleve. Kampfgruppe Peiper descended down the hill in the middle distance towards the bridge. *(Airborne Forces Museum)*

Company, and 11 Company had suffered heavy casualties and lost its commander, Obersturmführer Hasse, a holder of the Knight's Cross. By the end of the day the battalion had been driven back some distance, but held on to an area of the Coreu Forest called Six Moines, which covered the approaches to the Petit Spai bridge, the only line of retreat available to the German forces on the north bank of the Ambleve.

The remnants of Schnellgruppe Knittel, west of Stavelot, also saw heavy fighting during the day, as one of its members, Helmut Merscher, recalled:

> We drove in a schwimmwagen [amphibious jeep] through the forest and field trails to the battalion command post. We had to stop next to a couple of houses; the command post was also there. Four American tanks attacked and we had to seek cover in a nearby basement. The basement was already filled with Landser [infantrymen]. The waiting and the rattling of the tracks and the shooting made me nervous. I returned to the schwimmwagen, where there were three panzerfausten. I put them under my arm. Then I saw the four tanks standing and firing. I ran, ducking down, through a trench and approached to within 60-70m of the tanks. I cocked a panzerfaust, aimed it at the largest, a Sherman, and pulled the trigger and it hit. The tank immediately blazed up. I marked the next tank, but, at the same moment, took fire and did not hit. I changed position, aimed and hit the next tank. Then the other two turned and left.

Towards evening the survivors of Knittel's battalion, who, after five days' fighting on the western edge of Stavelot, were pitifully few, were ordered to withdraw to the Farm Antoine on the Stavelot–Trois Ponts road. Here they found four of von Westernhagen's King Tigers, which had not managed to reach the main body of Kampfgruppe Peiper. Hansen's and Knittel's men dug in and prepared to hold their line of retreat at the Petit Spai bridge. There was little likelihood of any further advance in the area.

Chapter Eleven

24 DECEMBER 1944:
THE LONG WALK

General Harrison believed he would have another hard battle on the 24th. His plan was to attack La Gleize from a new direction – the north. So far the town had been attacked from the west, south-west, south, south-east, east and north-east, but not from the north. The 2nd Battalion, 119th IR, would swing to the north of the town and attack it from that direction. The 1st Battalion would continue its attack from the south and south-west, while TF McGeorge would attack from the east. The 3rd Battalion, 119th IR, and TF Jordan would demonstrate from the west. Peiper's position would be pressured from all sides.

Harrison's men attacked at first light, but met very little resistance, except for one group of about fifty Germans who were positioned in the woods to the north of La Gleize. It is difficult to establish why this group still held their

Knocked-out German armour. The picture shows a Mk IV and a Panther tank.
(Airborne Forces Museum)

A Panther and a Mk IV captured by the Americans. *(Airborne Forces Museum)*

positions. Perhaps they had never received the order to withdraw. After a brief fight the Americans cleared the position for the loss of only ten wounded. The attack continued into the town, and found only the rearguard left behind by Peiper; the main body of the kampfgruppe had gone. The rearguard made a poor job of destroying the remaining equipment, and the Americans reported many vehicles in working order. Most of the vehicles had ammunition on board, but few had any fuel. The Americans also relieved 170 prisoners, mostly from the 3/119th, captured when the Germans took Stoumont. The German rearguard and remaining wounded amounted to some 127 men. Captain Franklin Ferriss reported the capture of seven King Tigers, fifteen Panthers, six Mk IVs, eight armoured cars, seventy half-tracks, six self-propelled 150mm howitzers, six 75mm and 88mm anti-tank guns, two 75mm assault guns, six 120mm mortars and five 20mm anti-aircraft guns, although this number may be exaggerated.

While Harrison made his plans, Peiper began to gather his men together from their positions after dark on the 23rd. The men were ordered to leave their positions in small groups and gather in the town, as Rottenführer Herman Staritz of 13 Company, Pz.Gren.Regt. 2, reported:

> I was a runner. We received orders to break out between 1700 and 1800 hours. At 1800 the first ones started out, always only two to four men at long intervals. We assembled up on the mountain. The drivers and those detailed to demolition work stayed behind. The GIs were continuously shooting into La Gleize. When we were then all on the mountain – it was already after midnight – the demolitions began. When the last of our demolitions had gone off we began to march, single file.

A small rearguard of wounded men and volunteers would remain behind to give the impression of the town being defended, and to carry out the destruction of all remaining vehicles using grenades and demolition charges. Of the 3,000 men of the kampfgruppe that had crossed the Ambleve at Stavelot, and the reinforcements they had received, only 800 men were fit to attempt the long march back to the safety of German lines. Karl Wortmann recalled the order to join the column:

> The night from 23rd to 24th December brought snow and frost. As on all previous nights, we stayed at our panzers. Suddenly there was a shout – or was I only dreaming? I heard the words 'Merry Christmas' – But Christmas wasn't until tomorrow, I replied. 'No, immediately' I was told. Then I understood! I mobilized my crew. It took only a few seconds before we realized what was going on. A few hand grenades were stuffed in my pocket; I grabbed my pistol and machine pistol. Whether the demolition charges that I left in the engine compartment of the panzer and in the geschutze actually went off, I do not know. We walked cross-country towards La Gleize. The engineer positions were also abandoned. Fortunately, after going a couple of hundred metres, we reached the column. We couldn't hear them; they were as quiet as mice, even though there were 800 men.

Hal McCown also commented on the march discipline of the column: 'The

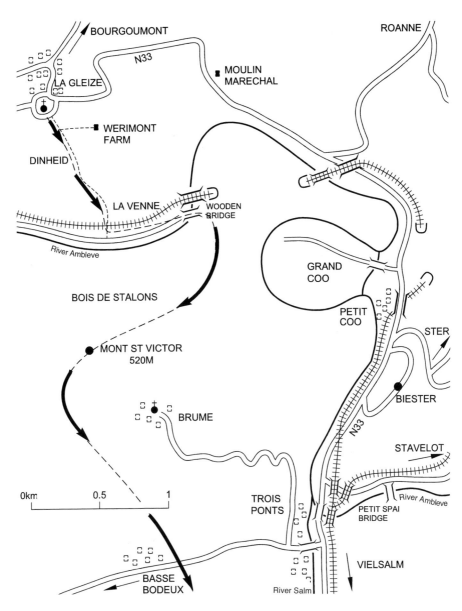

KG Peiper's escape route (1).

La Gleize. From the village square the remnants of the kampfgruppe started their long breakout march down the lane to the left, towards the Werimont Farm and the Ambleve footbridge at La Venne.

noise made by the entire 800-man group was so little that we could have passed within 200 yards of an outpost without detection.' The men were exhausted and hungry, but had a rough time ahead of them. The route led south from La Gleize over a hill known as Dinheid before dropping down to the Ambleve River at La Venne. Here two Belgian civilians, hiding in a cellar, were 'volunteered' to act as guides through the Bois de Stalons ahead of the column. After crossing the Ambleve by a small footbridge next to a railway viaduct the guides pointed the way up the steep slopes of the forest. For the march out, Peiper had distributed his officers throughout the column to encourage the men during the coming ordeal, and had also sent out small reconnaissance patrols to check the route for American forces in the way. Karl Wortmann described the rigours of the march:

> Our route led through a small ravine-like valley past several houses, then over
> a small wooden bridge that crossed the Ambleve and led us to a steep rocky
> mountain forest. This narrow forest trail used up our last ounces of strength.
> Our knees trembled to the point of near collapse, but we had to hold on. After

some time we reached a hill and were allowed to pause to catch our breath. My gaze wandered back through the valley, there, where the town of La Gleize lay, we saw only a burning tomb. Obersturmbannführer Peiper walked along the column right to the last man. He encouraged everyone. From exhaustion, almost all of the men lay under the trees on the cold ground. The pause lasted a good quarter of an hour. Then we continued. The route led us further up the mountains.

Herman Staritz is very much in agreement with Karl Wortmann, as to both the rigours of the march and Peiper's role in encouraging the men:

While we were on the march, Peiper occasionally went down the line to the men, encouraging them. We moved, all 800 men, in single file and I had an MG42 to carry, as we had brought all the crew served weapons with us. Otherwise, we were only able to take the most necessary items. I didn't freeze because I worked

Dinheid feature, looking back towards La Gleize. The kampfgruppe crossed this area as it began its breakout.

La Venne. The railway viaduct and footbridge over the Ambleve at La Venne. Peiper's 800 survivors crossed the bridge before disappearing into the Bois de Stalons.

up a good sweat going uphill, and it was up and down all the time. I would have done anything for Peiper; he was such a great example. Whenever we were in a bad spot – and I was really afraid – he always got us out of danger.

As the column wound its way up the steep tracks the sound of explosions came from below them, as Hal McCown reported:

At 05:00 we heard the first tank blow up and inside thirty minutes the entire area formally occupied by Colonel Peiper's command was a sea of fiercely burning vehicles, the work of the small detachment he had left behind to complete the destruction of his equipment.

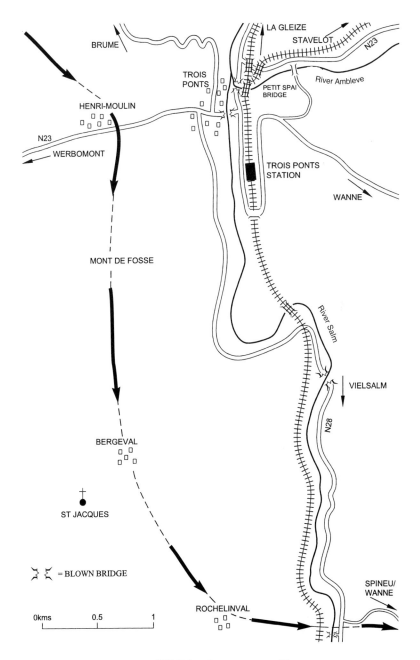

KG Peiper's escape route (2).

Other sources put the start of the explosions at 06:00. Peiper had ordered that the explosions would be staggered and would seem to the surrounding American troops as part of their continuing bombardment of the town.

Daylight found the kampfgruppe high on the slopes of Mont St Victor, from where Peiper could see that the bridge they were heading for had been blown. By this time Max Hansen's men had been forced back to the woods above the Petit Spai bridge, so crossing at the intended point would have put Peiper back among the American troops he was attempting to escape from. He was also aware that it would not take the Americans long to discover that the town had been abandoned, and for them to put up reconnaissance planes to search out the column. Peiper decided to conceal his men in the thick forest while his reconnaissance patrols looked for an alternative route. Hal McCown stated that he accompanied Peiper on one of these patrols. A patrol detected the presence of Americans in Brume, and it was decided to make a detour to the west to avoid the enemy. Karl Wortmann continues his account:

The route led us further up the mountains. Forward, with the lead element, was an American Major, McCown. He was being taken with us as a prisoner of war. After several hours we found ourselves in the Ardennes mountains. All of the men were at the end of their strength, but everyone picked themselves up in order to avoid captivity. We staggered from weakness and hunger, but we all had one ambition: to get out of this damned mess. That would be our greatest present on that day – Christmas Eve 1944. Meanwhile, it had become afternoon and we were taking another short rest. Almost everyone lay beneath the tall spruces.

The escape route would now take the kampfgruppe south, cutting across the N23, the main Trois Ponts to Basse Bodeux road, then south-east through the Bois Monte de Fosse, to Bergeval, before descending into the Salm River valley close to Rochelinval. Fording the river would then take the kampfgruppe into the safety of friendly lines. As darkness fell the exhausted German soldiers prepared to continue their march. Hal McCown sets the time at 17:00 hrs. Karl Wortmann continues his account of the breakout:

We re-formed into a long column. It was already dark. The narrow path led ever upward. Now and then we took another pause to catch our breath. The men would then automatically lay down on the bare ground from exhaustion. There was another pause that was decidedly longer than the previous. One of the officers, a Hauptsturmführer, came forward from the rear to see how things were going. It turned out that the column had separated. The Hauptsturmführer quickly made the decision to take command of the column. Reconnaissance patrols were dispatched to reconnoitre possible obstacles. I was part of one of these reconnaissance patrols. There was an open snow-covered slope in front of us. The path led further to the left along the edge of the forest and then bent to the right. The end of the forest was in the shape of a triangle. Suddenly, we were standing in the middle of an asphalt road. It led from Trois Ponts to Basse Bodeux. We heard and saw nothing! The Americans were celebrating

Christmas! We fetched the main body of the column. It went down the mountain to the road. We had to cross it. When we reached the point of the forest triangle, American soldiers suddenly jumped from the forest and pulled several of us into the bushes. The comrades behind us fired into the tip of the forest. This frightened the Americans and they set us loose, but then a wild shoot-out occurred which so frightened our column that they scattered in panic. The fight with the Americans lasted perhaps 20 minutes. Several comrades were wounded. Our leader, who quickly recognized the muddle, continued to shout: 'Stay together, don't split up' and ordered 'Reassemble!' We crossed the road in a unified dash and ended up in a deep ditch. Everyone took a deep breath. The wounded were hastily treated. One was shot by a rifle through the right shoulder, another had a graze in the upper thigh. We still had not yet recovered from the fight when we heard a vehicle approaching. We stayed dead still! Slowly, an American reconnaissance vehicle drove past us. No wonder the

The abandoned 69-ton King Tiger *332* barely fitted on the US M9 Tank Transporter. It was removed to the States for evaluation at the Aberdeen Proving Ground, Maryland. It is now on display at the Patton Museum of Cavalry and Armour, Fort Knox, Kentucky.

Americans were looking for us! It was over 20 hours since we had broken out of La Gleize with 800 men. The enemy knew we couldn't have just disappeared from the face of the earth! The Americans knew that if we wanted to reach friendly lines we had to cross two rivers, the Ambleve and the Salm. We waited a brief moment, then we continued in single file like a kommando. It was clear that the Americans were on our heels. The wounded were passed from comrade to comrade with great effort.

The column had split into two sections, whether by intention or accident is difficult to ascertain. Hal McCown was with Peiper's group, and reported that Peiper seemed to be lost:

I could tell then that Colonel Peiper was basing his direction of movement on the explosion of American artillery fire as the probable location of his friendly forces. His information as to the present front lines of both sides was as meagre as my own as he had no radio and no other outside contact. He continuously consulted his map, indicating that he was quite thoroughly lost. We continued moving from that time on continuously up and down the rugged hills, crossing small streams, pushing through thick undergrowth and staying off and away from roads and villages. At around 22:00 Colonel Peiper, his Executive and his S3 disappeared from the forward command group. I and my two guards were placed in charge of the regimental surgeon, whose familiar Red Cross bundle on his back made it easy for me to walk behind.

The strain of the past week seems to have affected Peiper, and McCown continues:

I tried in vain to find out where Colonel Peiper went; one friendly enlisted man of Colonel Peiper's headquarters told me that Colonel Peiper was very tired, and I believe that he and a few selected members of his staff must have holed up in some isolated house for food and rest, to be sent for from the main body after they had located friendly forces. The change of command of the unit also wrought a change in method of handling the men. A young captain in charge of the leading company operated very close to me and my knowledge of Latin as well as the German I had picked up enabled me to understand to some degree practically every order he issued. I heard him tell my guards to shoot me if I showed the slightest intention of escaping, particularly when we neared the Americans. Whereas Colonel Peiper had given a rest break every hour or so, there were no breaks given under the new command from that time until I escaped. The country we were now passing through was the most rugged we had yet encountered. All the officers were continuously exhorting the men to greater effort and to laugh at weakness. I was not carrying anything except my canteen, which was empty, but I know from my own physical reaction how tired the men with heavy weapons loads must have been. I heard repeated again and again the warning that if any man fell behind the tail of the column he would be shot. I saw some men crawling on hands and knees. I saw others who were wounded but who were being supported by comrades up the steep slopes; there were fully two dozen wounded in the column, the majority of whom were going along quite well by themselves. There was one captain who was rather severely

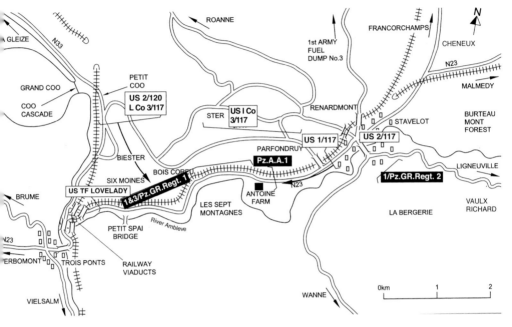

Fighting around Stavelot, 24 December 1944.

wounded, the Colonel had told me, who moved along supported by another officer and a medical NCO and was still with the unit the last time I saw him. We approached very close to where artillery fire was landing and the point pushed into American lines three times and turned back. I believe the Germans had several killed in these attempts.

The new leader of McCown's group became lost and a number of short discussions were held with other officers. By now it was midnight, and as the clock passed into Christmas Day the men were so exhausted that a decision was made to find shelter in a small village. At 01:00 a message came down the column that a suitable village, Bergeval, was just ahead. As the Germans approached the village, all hell let loose, as Hal McCown describes:

At this time I was not forward near the point, my guards held me back near the position which was occupied by the covering force between the village and the west, that is to say, towards the American rear. The outpost had already moved into position before firing broke out not very far from where I was standing. My guards and I hit the ground, tracer bullets flashed all around us, and we could hear the machine gun bullets cutting the trees very close to us. The American unit which I later found out was a company, drove forward again to clear what it obviously thought was a stray patrol, this time using mortar fire as well. The mortar fire fell all around the German position. I do not know if my guards were

*injured or not; shrapnel cut the trees all around us. The American machine gun
and rifle fire was very superior to that of the covering force. I could hear
commands being shouted in both German and English with the latter
predominating. There was considerable movement around me in the darkness. I
lay still for some time waiting for one of my guards to give me a command.
After some time I arose cautiously and began to move at right angles from the
direction of the American attack watching carefully to my rear to see if anyone
was covering or following me. After moving approximately 100 yards I turned
and moved directly toward the direction from which the American attack had
come. I can remember that I whistled some American tune; I have forgotten
which one it was. I had not gone over 200 yards before I was challenged by an
American outpost of the 82nd Airborne Division.*

General Gavin had ordered the 505th PIR to withdraw from the area of the
Salm River and Trois Ponts, and it was with this unit that the Germans
clashed. Sergeant Bill Dunfee was a member of I Company, and present when
Hal McCown was challenged by the American patrol:

*It was a cold, moonlit night with good visibility. It was too light to suit us. Ray
(Mike) Maikowski was out with the point. Mike noticed movement alongside
the road and eased the safety off his M1. The man hiding there made his
presence known, claiming to be an American.*

*Mike told him, 'Put your hands behind your head and get your ass out here
where I can see you.' It was an American, Major Hal McCown of the 30th
Infantry Division. After he got over his fright – he was sure Maikowski was
about to shoot him, and, knowing Mike, his fright was justified – he told us he
had been a prisoner of the 500 to 800 Germans that charged through our lines
earlier.*

Hal McCown was safely back with an American unit. One group of Germans
had broken through the withdrawing Americans and safely crossed the Salm.
Karl Wortmann's group also reached the Salm:

*The Salm could not be that far away. Reconnaissance patrols discovered that all
of the bridges were sharply watched by the Americans. Several enemy tanks
stood on the far side of the river bridges. More climbing. The lead elements made
another contact with the enemy. American machine guns could be heard
nearby, then there were cries from the comrades that were hit. A call went up,
everyone was to climb down the hill! The Salm valley was in front of us! What
were we to do now? Everyone who could swim was to climb down. Not many
reported in that cold. Most of the comrades sat along a high standing railroad
bed. Three metres below us we saw the rushing water of the Salm. The foam
sprayed a cold shower down our backs. We then had to make our way over the
stones that some hearty comrades laid in the ice-cold water. A human chain was
assembled and each was pulled up to the next, from stone to stone, sometimes
waist-deep in water, to the far bank. These 30-35 metres seemed to be endless to
us. Several times the chain was broken when comrades stumbled from the
stones. Day was already dawning as the last man reached the other bank. We*

walked along the road several hundred metres in the direction of Grand Halleux, then turned onto a narrow path that led directly up a steep rise. When we reached the top we found ourselves in no man's land and felt as good as if we were secure. After several kilometres through a forest we saw the town of Wanne where our units were located. It was the afternoon of the First Day of Christmas.

Herman Staritz was a member of the same group:

On the first day of Christmas – it was already light – we reached the Salm. We had to go through it, since the Americans were at the bridge waiting for us. The water was ice cold, in some places up to your chest. I had my MG on my shoulder and was holding the man in front of me by his jacket. That way each man had a hold on the next. As we emerged, all our belongings had frozen stiff, and then came the way – almost an hour – uphill to Wanne.

Reaching the safety of the German lines must have been one of the best Christmas presents that the members of the kampfgruppe ever received. Of the 800 men who crept out of La Gleize, 770 were present when the roll was called later on Christmas Day. It reflects on the discipline of the men and the efforts of their officers that only thirty men had been lost during the 20-kilometre march, which lasted thirty-six hours. Peiper made it safely across the Salm, and established his headquarters at Petit Thier.

While Peiper's men were carrying out their long walk back to the safety of German lines, the survivors of Kampfgruppe Hansen and Schnellgruppe Knittel were still fighting for their lives on the north bank of the Amblève. The American plan for the 24th was a continuation of the attack on the 23rd. Lieutenant Colonel Cantey's 2nd Battalion, 120th IR, with L Company of the 117th IR, would continue the attack towards the Amblève, while the 1/117th would push west along the line of the railroad from Stavelot. Cantey's attack would be preceded by an artillery barrage commencing at 08:45, and the infantry would begin their attack at 09:00. There were problems from the start of the advance. The supporting artillery did not fire the softening-up barrage, and Cantey was unable to stop his infantry advancing. The German troops put up a fierce resistance and the American advance ground to a halt. In an attempt to get the advance moving again the American artillery fired a number of TOT (Time on Target) missions. This required all the participating batteries to fire in such a manner that all the shells landed at exactly the same time, no matter what the range to the target. In a multi-battery shoot, the shells from the closest battery arrived first, allowing the enemy troops to take cover. This was not the case with a TOT mission as all the shells arrived simultaneously with little warning. They could be devastating. The fire missions made the situation worse, as half the shells landed on the American infantry, particularly F Company, 2/120th. During the course of the day the Americans advanced a mere 300 yards.

G Company, 2/120th, had been tasked with pushing down the river road and relieving the elements of TF Lovelady that were holding the area around the railway viaduct at Trois Ponts. The day proved to be a disaster, as the company ran into German tanks and suffered heavy casualties – five killed, twenty-four wounded and seven missing. The company was so depleted that it was withdrawn from action to recuperate.

During the afternoon the 2nd Battalion of the 119th IR arrived, fresh from the capture of La Gleize, to reinforce Lieutenant Colonel Cantey's force. Task Force Lovelady was withdrawn and recombined with the other task forces of CCB. The Combat Command then returned to its parent division, 3rd Armoured.

Preparations were made to continue the attack on Christmas Day, and Captain Franklin Ferriss sums up its results:

A very careful plan of attack was worked out and put into execution. But, when the troops moved in for the kill, they found, as they had at La Gleize, that the enemy had pulled out the previous night. Practically no prisoners were taken on either side during the three days of this battle in the woods.

By nightfall on 25 December the 30th Division held a continuous line along the north bank of the Ambleve. All surviving members of the Leibstandarte had pulled back south of the river. The fighting around Stavelot had been fierce. Kampfgruppe Hansen had lost over 500 men during the attempt to relieve Peiper, while Schnellgruppe Knittel had lost almost 300. American casualties had been high with 65 killed, 174 wounded and 63 missing. It was also reported that 142 Belgian civilians had lost their lives, and several more would do so from the injuries they had suffered.

By the close of Christmas Day Kampfgruppe Peiper's trial by fire was over. Its members had still to suffer another trial.

Chapter Twelve

TRIALS AND RETRIBUTION

Kampfgruppe Peiper had failed in its mission to capture the Meuse crossings and push on to Antwerp. There were a number of reasons for this failure, and with the aid of hindsight it seems apparent that they were doomed to failure from the start. It is worth considering the factors that contributed to the failure of Peiper's mission. Firstly, the Leibstandarte's running mate in 1st SS Panzer Corps, the 12th SS Panzer Division Hitler Jugend, had failed to penetrate the American lines. It was intended that they should proceed along the northern routes, widening the breakthrough and protecting the northern flank of the Leibstandarte. A courageous American defence of the twin

American troops examine a King Tiger. Many of the kampfgruppe's tanks had to be abandoned when they ran out of fuel. *(Airborne Forces Museum)*

villages of Krinkelt and Rocherath held up the Hitler Jugend's advance long enough for a strong defensive line to be formed to the west of the villages – a line the Germans were unable to penetrate. Had the Hitler Jugend broken through as planned, the 30th Division troops that held Malmedy, recaptured Stavelot and eventually defeated Peiper, would have entered the battle further to the north, and would not have been in place to stop the kampfgruppe at Stoumont station. At this stage of the battle the American forces were badly stretched and it is difficult to see where other reinforcements could have been found to stop the 6th Panzer Army reaching the Meuse.

Another contributing factor was the terrain through which Peiper had to advance. For most of the way the kampfgruppe was restricted to the roads, due to the hilly, heavily wooded terrain. For much of the advance, Peiper's men attacked on a frontage of a single vehicle, and his column stretched for 25km. Sixty years on, it is still difficult to negotiate some of these roads in a family car, let alone a Tiger or Panther tank, and it is a wonder that the kampfgruppe made the progress that it did!

Peiper also had to cross a number of rivers along his route – the Ambleve, the Salm and the Lienne. There were few bridges across these rivers that were strong enough for tanks to cross, and small bodies of American combat engineers were able to delay or even halt the progress of the kampfgruppe. On the night of the 17th, with Stavelot virtually unoccupied, a squad of engineers, equipped with small arms and one bazooka, put enough doubt

The spoils of war: captured German equipment. In the picture can be seen two towed 105mm howitzers, an armoured car, a Panther, a Mk III tank and an assortment of wheeled transport. *(Airborne Forces Museum)*

into Peiper's mind that he halted the kampfgruppe until first light, which also gave his column time to close up. Although the bridge at Stavelot was successfully captured and elements of the kampfgruppe crossed the Ambleve and pushed on, the Americans were able to recapture the town and eventually blew the bridge, blocking any further vehicular reinforcements reaching Peiper. On the 18th the Americans blew three bridges as the Germans approached them. First was the Ambleve bridge at Trois Ponts, which was blown as Peiper approached it along the Stavelot-Trois Ponts road. Peiper had dispatched his two Mk IV companies along the south bank of the Ambleve to seize the Salm bridge, but once again this was demolished as the panzers approached. Finally, later in the day a squad of American engineers blew up the Lienne bridge, which forced Peiper to retrace his route back to La Gleize and then on to Stoumont the following day. On each occasion all that opposed the kampfgruppe – the most powerful in the German offensive – was a small body of American engineers, and these brave men should be given much of the credit for Peiper's defeat. How Peiper must have regretted not having a heavy bridging train with his column!

With the kampfgruppe as the spearhead of the advance, Peiper's supply column would not be able to keep pace with them, and Peiper expressed concerns about keeping his vehicles fuelled up. The kampfgruppe had 60km to drive to its first objective, the Meuse, which was well within the fuel range of all his vehicles. This does not take into account the road conditions, keeping engines running while stationary, and the massively increased fuel consumption once a unit gets into combat. Peiper had been ordered to refuel his tanks from captured American dumps, and he did this on a number of occasions. The Meuse should have been reached on the 17th, but with delays and having to retrace its route on a number of occasions, elements of the kampfgruppe were low on fuel by the time they reached Stavelot. Peiper's Mk IV companies – 6 and 7 – were so low on fuel after their push to Trois Ponts that they had to drain the fuels tanks of the bulk of the panzers to allow the remainder to push on towards La Gleize. As the Americans recaptured Stavelot and blew the bridge, the bulk of the two companies did not cross the Ambleve. After several days' fighting around Stoumont, La Gleize and Cheneux, the bulk of Peiper's vehicles were very low on fuel, and a number of accounts describe tanks having to be towed into position by other tanks. The Leibstandarte tried a number of ploys to get fuel through to the kampfgruppe. These included floating half-empty jerrycans down the Ambleve, sending a panzergrenadier battalion on foot carrying jerrycans, and even an attempted airdrop. None of these efforts alleviated the kampfgruppe's chronic fuel shortage, and the Americans reported that many of the vehicles captured at La Gleize had empty fuel tanks.

The three remaining kampfgruppen were drawn into attempts to break through to Peiper, but as the American 30th Division consolidated its positions around Peiper, at Stavelot, and between Peiper and Trois Ponts, it became increasingly unlikely that reinforcements would reach him. By 23 December the Germans attempting to push north along the Ambleve had been halted and were fighting for survival against increasing American opposition. Nothing remained but to withdraw the survivors back onto the south bank of the Ambleve, and on 25 December this was achieved.

This was not the end of the Leibstandarte's, or indeed the 1st SS Panzer Corps', involvement in the Ardennes offensive. Further south, around Bastogne, an important road-junction town, the 5th Panzer Army had succeeded where the 6th Panzer Army had failed. Although Bastogne was held by the 101st Airborne Division, and would not be captured by the Germans, the town had been surrounded and German panzer forces had

Bullingen churchyard after the battle.

bypassed the town, to both the north and south, and pushed on towards the Meuse. The furthest penetration was by the 2nd Panzer Division, whose reconnaissance elements had come within site of the Meuse before been halted and pushed back. General George Patton's 3rd Army, stationed south of the Ardennes, carried out a 90-degree turn to push north and relieve Bastogne, an amazing feat. The I and II SS Panzer Corps were moved to the Bastogne area, with the mission of cutting the corridor between Patton's forces and the 101st Airborne Division in Bastogne. They were unable to break through the American lines and were withdrawn to rebuild and refit. The Americans went onto the counteroffensive and slowly, but surely, drove the Germans back to their original start line as on 16 December, although it took most of January to do so.

The reconstituted Leibstandarte took part in the final German offensive of the war, the Lake Balaton offensive, an attempt to relieve the beleaguered garrison of Budapest. Although initially successful, the German offensive coincided with a major Russian attack to the north, which threatened to cut off the attacking German forces. In a hurried fighting retreat the bulk of the German forces managed to escape from the threatened pocket and pulled back into the wooded hills to the north, where they remained for the rest of the war. In a mad dash the Leibstandarte, including the survivors of Kampfgruppe Peiper, reached the American lines in Austria and crossed to the relative safety of the American zone, where they duly surrendered.

For some members of the kampfgruppe and the division their war was not yet over. They were incarcerated in Dachau in preparation for a war crimes trial. Over seventy members of the kampfgruppe and several senior officers, including Sepp Dietrich, were charged with the murder of between 538 and 749 unnamed prisoners and 90 unidentified Belgian civilians, although a number of members of the kampfgruppe were charged specifically with the murder of 72 members of Battery B at the Baugnez crossroads, which was increased to 84 as more bodies were recovered.

After a brief trial forty-two of the accused were sentenced to death by hanging; their request for a military execution by firing squad was turned down. Lieutenant Colonel Willis M. Everett, the defending officer, carried out a personal crusade to get the tribunal's decision overturned. There was some evidence that the testimony and confessions of many of the accused had been given under duress. Beatings, mock executions, threats and withholding of rations were among the list of methods used by the Americans to gain evidence, according to Everett, and the scandal went as far as a US Senate hearing, although the conclusion was that there was insufficient evidence to overturn the sentences.

Over a period of six years the forty-two death sentences given out by the tribunal were commuted to life imprisonment. By 1951 only Jochen Peiper and five others were still on death row, before their death sentences were also commuted. Peiper was the last member of the kampfgruppe to be freed from prison, after serving eleven years of his life sentence, fifty-five months of which were spent on death row. After his release from prison Peiper found

The body of a member of B Battery found when the Americans recaptured the Baugnez crossroads area.

civilian life very difficult. His wartime career continued to haunt him, with attempts to retry him for the Baugnez incident, and a fresh attempt to try him for an incident in Italy earlier in the war. Eventually Peiper and his wife settled in Traves in France, where a modicum of peace prevailed. This was shattered in June 1976 when a hate campaign including leaflets and graffiti was started against Peiper by French Left Wing anarchists. In early July the campaign intensified, and on the 13th Peiper received a letter telling him that his house would be burnt down. Peiper's wife, Sigi, left the house, but Peiper, a soldier to the last, stayed to defend his property. In the early hours of 14 July – Bastille Day – the local fire service was called to the house, which was well ablaze. A body, later identified as Peiper's, was found within the charred remains. When police examined the scene there was evidence of a fire fight having taken place, and three Molotov cocktails having been used to torch the house. After a long delay Peiper's body was released for burial, and was laid to rest in a family plot at Schondorf am Ammersee in Bavaria. His murderers were never found, and investigations are still ongoing.

The final volume of the semi-official history of the Leibstandarte Adolf Hitler (Tiemann, 1998) has a photograph of Peiper at the back, and a dedication stating that he was the last member of the division to die in combat.

BATTLEFIELD TOUR ROUTE

The following tour allows the reader to follow the route of Kampfgruppe Peiper. Throughout the tour, places of interest are pointed out. Details of the events along the route are given in the main text, and you should refer to this throughout the tour.

The nature of the terrain in the Ardennes region of Belgium and the distances involved in following Kampfgruppe Peiper's route make your own transport essential. Today the Ardennes is a tourist area, offering a multitude of recreational activities such as walking, cycling, canoeing, caving, climbing and skiing. It is covered by vast tracts of forests, cut through by steep valleys, meandering rivers and streams, and high moorland (the Hohes Venn). It is beautiful countryside with quaint towns and villages and its scenery attracts visitors from all over Europe.

Maps

To gain the most benefit from the tour, it would be useful to consult the following maps to your visit: the new IGN series 1:50,000, sheets 50-50A, and 49-49A. The older 1:25,000 maps, sheets 50/5-6 and 49/7-8 are of more use, if you can find a copy.

Travel

You are likely to arrive in the area by one of two routes: flying into Brussels (Zaventem Airport), where you can hire a car, or in your own car via the Channel Tunnel or the ferry to Calais. On exiting the tunnel or ferry port,

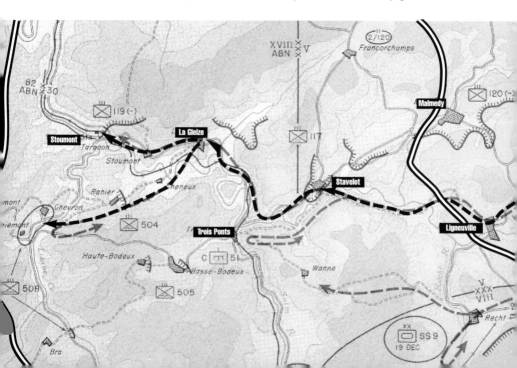

follow the signs for Brussels (E40). Anyone arriving at Zeebrugge continues on the same route, following the E40 to Brussels, via Bruges and Ghent. Once you approach the Brussels ring road, keep right following the signs for Aken (Aachen), Luik (Liege) and the airport (Zaventem). If you have hired a car in Brussels, join the E40 and drive east to Aken (Aachen). Bear in mind that in Belgium you could be confronted with three different names for the same place (Flemish, French and German). After passing Liege (Luik or Luttich!), but before arriving in the area of the kampfgruppe's operations, you may wish to visit one of the main American military cemeteries in the area, at Henri Chapelle, with 7,898 burials, many from the Ardennes battles. To get there, leave the E40 at the N3 turnoff. Once through Thermister-Clermont the road is signposted for the cemetery. At the same turnoff, those wishing to travel direct to the battle area should turn right onto the E42 south (St Vith/Prum). The E42 then divides between Malmedy and Stavelot, which are both tourist centres, and the Tourist Information offices in either town can help you find accommodation. You are now within the battlefield area.

The Battlefield Tour

The tour starts at the pleasant town of Blankenheim, situated in Nordrhein-Westfalen, Germany. Drive south from Blankenheim on the B51 (Reichstrasse 51 in 1944, now much wider than it was at the time of the battle), towards Stadtkyll. This area gives the visitor a good idea of the type of terrain through which the various kampfgruppen of the 1st SS Panzer Division made their

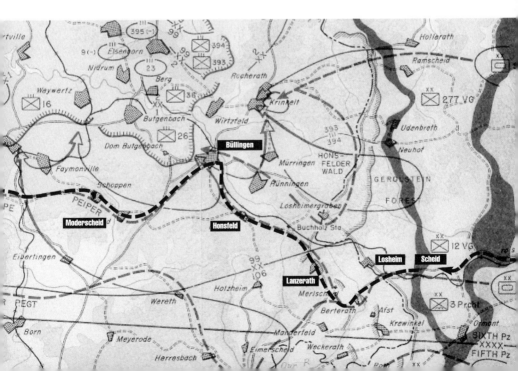

way forward to the battle area. Before reaching Stadtkyll, turn right on to Bundestrasse 261. This route, though much improved, gives some idea of the winding and twisting route that Kampfgruppe Peiper and the rest of the 1st SS Panzer Division had to take on its approach march to the battle area. After passing through Kronenberg and Hallschlag the kampfgruppe approached its first obstacle. This is the road bridge (B421) across the railway at Scheid. As you pass the last of the large wind-farm generators on your right, pull off the road and pause. This is the road bridge that was blown by the Germans in the September retreat. Some earlier books on Kampfgruppe Peiper state that this blown bridge was a major obstacle to their advance. In reality it created little hindrance to the kampfgruppe. Peiper directed his *spitze* down the track to the right of the bridge, which leads to a crossing over the railway. This allowed the *spitze* to continue its advance, closely followed by the rest of Peiper's kampfgruppe. From here drive west for a short distance along the B421 in the direction of Losheim, passing a timber yard on the left. At the T-junction with the B265 turn right. This road would have been Peiper's route onto Rollbahn C, towards Losheimergraben, but, because of the volksgrenadiers' failure to break through the American lines, the kampfgruppe was diverted.

Take the first left in the direction of St Vith. Almost immediately after turning you leave Germany and enter Belgium. The road begins a steep descent into the valley. Pause in the lay-by on the left, before a junction. It was along this road that the *spitze* encountered several minefields, and Obersturmführer Sternebeck lost two Panthers in quick succession. Looking out over the valley, take note of the small white church in the distance. Before Sternebeck reached this point his own tank was wrecked by a mine. Continue downhill into Belgium and then turn sharp right in the direction of Hullschied. This turn is much easier today than it was when the tanks, half-tracks and other vehicles of the kampfgruppe negotiated it during the darkness of the night of 17 December 1944. Keep left, turning uphill, in the direction of Merlscheid, passing the small white church, mentioned earlier, on your right.

Continue on the same road and at the junction with the N626, turn right in the direction of Lanzerath (2km). On entering the village, pause at the large building on the left, known today as the 'Calypso'. This building was the temporary headquarters of the commander of 9th Fallschirmjager Regiment, Oberst Hoffmann. It was in this building that Lyle Bouck witnessed a heated discussion between Hoffmann and Peiper, after the latter's arrival at around midnight on 16 December.

Continue driving north on N626, turning left in the direction of Bucholz/Honsfeld. Where the terrain opens up on your right is the area of Bucholz Station. Vehicular access is not permitted, but a short walk will take you to the station area. Continue on to where the road bears sharp left to Honsfeld. After about 500m you exit the wood line and enter farmland. Continue west, and a little further on, at a Y-junction, keep right in the direction of Honsfeld. Honsfeld was used as a rest and recuperation area by the US 99th Infantry Division. Peiper's men surprised and captured many American soldiers, complete with their vehicles.

From Honsfeld, press on in the direction of Bullingen. As you approach the town, the area to the left was an airfield at the time of the battle. At the Y-junction, Sternebeck and his *spitze* followed the road to the right. Follow this road to the crossroads and continue straight across with the church on your left. The road runs down the hill past a large factory on the right before reaching a junction. Turn left under the railway bridge, following the road out toward Rocherath. The road begins to bend to the right, and it was in this area that the *spitze* came under fire from American anti-tank guns in Wirtzfeld. Retrace your steps back to Bullingen and turn right at the crossroads. At the western end of Bullingen, turn left off the N632, in the direction of St Vith. Park by the trees on the left just before the *Gendarmerie*. The area to the left of the road was an American fuel depot where many of the kampfgruppe's vehicles were refuelled.

Continue along this road until you reach a roundabout. A short detour by turning right here will brings you to another roundabout, in the middle of which is a memorial to the US 1st Infantry Division who held the area around Dom Butgenbach. Parking is available on the left. Return the way you came back to the first roundabout. Turn right, taking the minor concrete road past the timber yards on both your left and right and continue on to Moderscheid. In the village, take the first right turn and drive downhill past the church. Make a right turn at the next junction in the direction of Schoppen. At Schoppen, take the left turn signposted Amel (Ambleve). At the next junction, turn right to Faymonville. At the western end of Faymonville, just past the sign for Schoppen, turn left onto a minor road. Follow this road past a large industrial unit on your right, then, a little further on, at a T-junction, turn left, which will take you past a farm entrance. As you drive past the next farmhouse (on the right), take the next right turn. Continue driving downhill, past a farm on the right, then take the second turn on the left, and follow the road down the hill into the village of Ondenvaal. In the village, turn right onto the N676 and take the first left in the direction of Thirimont. Continue driving uphill, past the cemetery on your right (outside the village) and follow the main road through Thirimont, passing the church on the right. At the western edge of the village, note the road that branches off to the left. This is where elements of Preuss's 10 Company attempted to take a short cut to the N62 (Malmedy–St Vith road). The route that Preuss attempted in December 1944, which was impassable then because of the mud, can be safely completed today in a sturdy 4 x 4.

Under pressure from Peiper, the *spitze* continued straight ahead along the main road you are travelling along. After a left-hand bend the road straightens out before continuing on to a T-junction. It is worth pausing a few hundred metres before this junction. Although new woodland to your left now blocks the view of the Malmedy–St Vith road, beyond the trees, Werner Sternebeck had a clear view of the road in 1944, and his men opened fire on the long enemy truck column over to their left. These trucks belonged to B

Battery, 285th Artillery Observation Battalion, and could be seen moving south along the Malmedy–St Vith road, approximately 1,000m away. Continue to the T-junction and turn left, following the signs for Malmedy. At the next major junction turn left onto the N62 towards St Vith. After about 200m, stop. You are now at Baugnez crossroads, the site of the infamous 'Malmedy massacre'. The new house behind you to the right stands close to the site of the massacre of the American prisoners. Opposite is the US memorial to those killed. On the other side of the road is the farm belonging to Henri Le Joly, who was one of only two civilian witnesses to the incident. The other, Madame Bodarwe, owned a café at the road junction, which has

Baugnez. The memorial to the American soldiers massacred at Baugnez crossroads. The name of each soldier is commemorated on a tablet on the wall.

Ligneuville. The memorial to the American soldiers murdered by the kampfgruppe in Ligneuville.

since been demolished.

Continue down the N62 in the direction of Ligneuville. As the road begins to descend and you approach the first major bend to the right, note the narrow track that joins you from the left. This is where the lane along which elements of Preuss's 10 Company tried to take a short cut, mentioned previously, joins the N62. Drive down the descent into Ligneuville and park on the right-hand side of the road before the Hotel du Moulin, just before the left-hand bend in the road. On the right is a memorial to US soldiers shot by the kampfgruppe in the village. Up the small road to the right of the memorial was the American dozer tank, in the town for repair, which knocked out Arndt Fischer's Panther tank when it rounded the bend by the hotel, as Peiper's command element entered the village, following the *spitze*. The Hotel du Moulin was US Brigadier General Timberlake's command post, which he and his staff managed to vacate only minutes before the Germans arrived in the village. This hotel is well graded and, as with most top restaurants in the Ardennes region, its menu offers many local game and fish dishes, complemented by some excellent wines.

Continue through the village, crossing the Ambleve river bridge, and at the top of the hill take the right-hand turn in the direction of Vielsalm/Pont on the N660. It is worth noting that this road was used by all the vehicles of the kampfgruppe, including the King Tigers of the 501st Heavy Tank Battalion – little imagination is required to picture how difficult it would have been to negotiate this narrow, twisting and winding road in tanks and half-tracks, particularly in the failing light. Pass through the village of Pont and under the viaduct carrying the modern E42. Take the next right in the direction of Stavelot, keeping off the E42. It is a drive of approximately six kilometres to Vaulx Richard. Continue a few hundred metres from the village along the Stavelot road. As the road begins to descend prior to reaching the rock outcrop, note the small moss-covered stone foundation to the left of the road. Pull over at this point, but take care while parking. This is the spot where Private Bernie Goldstein challenged the lead vehicles of the kampfgruppe on the evening of 17 December 1944 – neither side knew how many enemies confronted them, and while Goldstein carried out a 'strategic withdrawal', the kampfgruppe came to a halt. Further down the hill the remaining members of Goldstein's engineer squad had set up a roadblock, before they too withdrew down the hill into Stavelot. Continue down the hill and stop where the road straightens out. The view across Stavelot and the Ambleve valley is stunning. Note the road across the valley, running out of Stavelot, left to right. It was from this road that American M-10 tank destroyers engaged the kampfgruppe on the morning of 18 December as the column descended in single file into Stavelot.

Continue down the hill towards Stavelot until the older red-brick houses on the right are reached. These houses still bear the scars of the kampfgruppe's passage, with the marks of numerous bullet strikes still being visible. Closer to the bottom of the hill (opposite house number 13) is a small monument to US forces on the left-hand side of the road. Pause here. Leave your car and continue on foot down the hill to another monument that commemorates the civilians murdered by the kampfgruppe in and around Stavelot. Return to your car and drive towards the river, parking on the right-hand side of the road. It was here that one of the King Tigers of 501st Heavy Tank Battalion was abandoned because of a mechanical failure. On the left-hand side of the road is an American M3 half-track. Cross over the bridge. Note the panels inlaid in the bridge parapet. Peiper's tanks crashed through the American defences on this side of the bridge and careered on through Stavelot, before continuing towards Trois Ponts. Walk up the cobbled streets towards the centre of town until you reach the Rue de la Haut Rivage on your left. As well as traversing the main square of Stavelot, this was another route that that

Stavelot. The memorial commemorating all the American soldiers killed during the defence of Stavelot.

Stavelot. The memorial to all the American units which defended Stavelot. The M3 half-track stands on the south bank of the Ambleve.

the kampfgruppe could have taken to reach the Trois Ponts road. Many of the buildings on the Haut Rivage show evidence of the battle, with bullet holes around their windows. This is also where one of von Westernhagen's King Tigers rolled back down the street and badly damaged two of the houses. The resulting rebuilding can be clearly seen.

Return to your car and drive across the bridge past the abbey entrance on your right. Because of a change in traffic priorities it is no longer possible to drive on the exact route the kampfgruppe took through the town. Be careful while driving on the cobbled streets as there are no road markings at junctions. When you reach the crossroads, with the town square ahead of you, turn right. Drive on, past the numerous cafes and restaurants on the left, and continue straight ahead at the mini traffic island, until you reach a roundabout (about 300m). Turn left onto the N23 towards Trois Ponts. As you begin to leave Stavelot, note how the ground rises on your right toward the villages of Ster, Parfondruy and Francorchamps. In 1944 the kampfgruppe would have exited the town past the railway station, and turned left towards Trois Ponts.

Continue along the N23 in the direction of Trois Ponts, pausing after 1km opposite a large red-brick farmhouse on the left. This is Antoine Farm, which served as the command post of the Panzer Reconnaissance Battalion's commander, Sturmbannführer Gustav Knittel, during the attacks towards the western edge of Stavelot. Note the battle scars on the east gable of the house.

Continue in the direction of Trois Ponts. Just over 2km further is the Petit Spai bridge, on the left of the road, by the bus stop. Park here. The track that leads across the bridge eventually joins up with the Wanne–Trois Ponts road. Walk up the track a short distance towards the river. It was across the bridge in front of you that the Leibstandarte's Panzerjagers attempted to cross the Ambleve and reinforce the attempted breakthrough to Peiper in La Gleize. Unfortunately, the bridge collapsed as the first vehicle tried to cross, and both bridge and Panzerjager plunged into the river. A makeshift bridge was built by the German engineers, but it could only accommodate foot traffic. This allowed the panzergrenadiers of Max Hansen's regiment to cross the river and attempt to lift the siege. Turn back towards the road. It was in the Bois de Coreu, the wooded hills in front of you, that the panzergrenadiers battled with US soldiers of the 30th Division. Return to your car.

Continue under the railway viaducts and turn left in the direction of Hamoir N66/Vielsalm N68. Cross

Stavelot. Memorial to the 596th Parachute Engineer Company on the north side of the Stavelot Bridge.

the bridge, turn around and drive back over and stop on the north side. Note the plaque on the wall of the bridge commemorating the participation of C Company, 51st Engineer Combat Battalion, in the defence of Trois Ponts, and the memorial to Belgian civilians killed in the area. It was the blowing of this bridge over the Ambleve River that forced Peiper to turn right after emerging from the railway viaducts onto the N33 towards Stoumont/La Gleize.

As you enter the village of Petit Coo, note further reminders of battle on the bullet-ridden gable end of the red-brick house opposite the garage.

Continue on the N63 in the direction of Liege/Remouchamps, through Grand Coo. As you pass under the railway viaduct a road joins from the right. This is the road from Roanne, where Task Force Lovelady entered the fray, severing Peiper from his supply route through Stavelot. Further along this road (approximately 700m) the group of buildings on the right is close to the site of Moulin Marechal, which was held by the Germans as a strongpoint during the early part of the fighting around La Gleize. Continue up the hill into La Gleize. Take the second left turn, which is signed 'Rahier 7', down a short lane. It was in this lane that the Americans tested the armour of a captured King Tiger with their bazookas. At the T-junction at the bottom of the lane turn right. Note the impressive building in the trees ahead. This is the Chateau Froid Cour, and was the home of the De Harenne family. The chateau and its estate buildings featured prominently during the fighting around Stoumont and La Gleize.

Follow the winding road to a crossroads, where you continue straight on. Take care at the crossroads as there are no priority signs. As you emerge from the woods there is a clear view to your right across the Ambleve river

Trois Ponts. Commemorative plaque on the Ambleve road bridge at Trois Ponts, to C Company, 51st ECB, who blew the bridge in Peiper's face on 18 December 1944.

bridge to Cheneux, at the top of the hill. Drive over the bridge, where there is parking on the left. Continue uphill towards the village pausing at the first right-hand bend. It was in this area, as the lead vehicles of the kampfgruppe approached Cheneux, that they were subjected to a sustained air attack by US fighter-bombers, and lost a number of tanks and other vehicles.

Continue uphill into Cheneux, and note the view across the Ambleve valley to the Chateau Froid Cour. Park near the church. Note the plaque to 504th Parachute Infantry of the 82nd Airborne Division and the memorial to Belgian civilians. Drive on to Rahier and then through Froidville to the junction with the N66. Turn right and continue downhill in the direction of the E25 over the Lienne River at the Neufmoulin bridge. Pause on the left-hand side of the road once you have crossed the bridge. Here can be seen a memorial stone to 291st Engineer Combat Battalion. It was members of this unit that blew the bridge in Peiper's face, as he approached it at dusk on 18

Cheneux. Memorial to
the 504th PIR close to the
church in Cheneux.

Lienne Bridge.
Commemorative plaque
to the men of the 291st
ECB who blew the bridge
in the face of the
advancing kampfgruppe
on 18 December 1944.

December 1944, prompting him to exclaim 'Those damned engineers!'. Peiper then dispatched panzergrenadier patrols from his 10 and 11 Companies north along the river to locate further crossing points.

Turn around and return in the direction of Rahier/Froidville. Take the second turning to the left, marked 'Chauveheid'. Follow the road down to the river and stop at the small stone bridge at Les Forges, which was reached by a patrol of 11 Company. This bridge could take the weight of SPWs but not tanks. Return through Chauveheid, then turn right onto the N66. Turn left back towards Froidville/Rahier and Cheneux. In Froidville, just before the road bends right, turn left, follow this road north for 500m and turn left again. Following the road down into the valley, turn left to the bridge at Moulin de Rahier. This bridge too was incapable of taking the weight of Peiper's tanks, but it did not stop SPWs from crossing and moving south-west along the opposite side of the river until they reached the village of Oufny, where they clashed with elements of the 2nd Battalion, 119th IR, and were forced to turn back.

Now follow in the kampfgruppe's footsteps and retrace your route through Cheneux and the Ambleve river bridge. Peiper left a garrison in Cheneux to protect this crossing. The remainder of kampfgruppe recrossed the river bridge and headed back to La Gleize. After about a kilometre you will reach a small crossroads. Turn left, through the woods. Note the estate farm buildings on your left, which served as Peiper's command post during the attack towards Stoumont. At the junction with the main road (N33) turn left in the direction of Stoumont, although this is not signposted. A short distance along this route is the main entrance to Chateau Froid Cour. The lodge house served as Werner Poetschke's command post during the battle for Stoumont.

As the N33 turns to the right as it approaches Stoumont, keep an eye out for the brick *Gendarmerie* on the left with an antenna on its roof.

Rochelinval. Memorial
to the 551st Parachute
Infantry Battalion.

Furthest point. Stone marker raised by the Cycling Club of Belgium at the point of the kampfgruppe's furthest advance. Other stones were raised at the furthest advance points of the German forces throughout the Ardennes.

Park near the church on the left and walk back along the road. The half-timbered house after the *Gendarmerie* existed in 1944 and features prominently in film and photographs taken during the battle for Stoumont. In this film, German fallschirmjager are clearly seen setting an MG42 in the small field where the Gendarmerie now stands. In the same film, Werner Poetschke can be seen turning around to pick up a discarded panzerfaust anti-tank weapon.

Continue west on N33 and note the former sanatorium (the large building) off to your right as the road exits the village. Continue driving out of Stoumont to Targnon. After approximately 1.5km there is a turnoff on the left signposted 'Ferme des Abompres' – Zabompre Farm. Park here. This can be a busy road during the tourist season, so beware of traffic. Walk from where you parked to the stone marker on the left side of the road. This was the 'high watermark' for Peiper on the early afternoon of 19 December. Turn around to face back towards Stoumont. The bend in the road is the furthest point that the kampfgruppe reached. On the bend the three lead Panthers of the kampfgruppe were knocked out and the advance halted. From here, there were now no other routes out of the Ambleve valley. Note how restricted the road is, with the river and the railway on your left and the high gradient and forest on your right. As they were able to advance on only a single vehicle frontage this was a panzer commander's nightmare!

Turn around and drive back to Stoumont. Stop at the entrance to the village by the driveway to the Sanatorium St Edouard. This building suffered extensive damage during the American attacks to recapture the village.

Drive back to La Gleize and turn right in the village towards the 'December 1944 Museum'. You are confronted by the most impressive monument left on the Ardennes battlefield, the King Tiger that was commanded by Obersturmführer Dollinger, commander of von Westernhagen's 2 Company. You have driven along the roads taken by these huge 70-ton monsters, and one cannot help agreeing with Peiper's comment that 'It's a route for bicycles, let alone tanks', when he learnt of his role in the operation.

La Gleize. The December 1944 Museum in the village square at La Gleize. Obersturmfuhrer Dollinger's King Tiger is on permanent display.

The Breakout

Park in the village square of La Gleize, where the troops gathered for the breakout in the early hours of Christmas Eve 1944. Follow the lane down to your right past the King Tiger tank. Continue towards Werimont Ferme. The meadow to your left contained the bulk of the destroyed or abandoned SPWs and guns of the kampfgruppe. Turn right at the next junction. You are now walking over the eastern side of the Dinheid feature. The lane drops down in to the Ambleve valley. Continue under the railway bridge and turn left, towards La Venne. Continue along the road until you reach a small road bridge and a railway viaduct. It was over this bridge that the 800 remaining survivors crossed the Ambleve before disappearing into the Bois de Stalons. It would take them thirty-six hours to reach and cross the Salm River and reach the safety of German lines. Retrace your steps back to your car in La Gleize.

Appendix A

SS Ranks and their US and British equivalents

SS Ranks and their British and US equivalents

Waffen SS		British Army	US Army
SS-*Brigadeführer*		Brigadier	Brigadier General
SS-*Oberführer*		(not applicable)	Senior Colonel
SS-*Standartenführer*		Colonel	Colonel
SS-*Obersturmbannführer*		Lieutenant Colonel	Lieutenant Colonel
SS-*Sturmbannführer*		Major	Major
SS-*Hauptsturmführer*		Captain	Captain
SS-*Obersturmführer*		Lieutenant	1st Lieutenant
SS-*Untersturmführer*		2nd Lieutenant	2nd Lieutenant
SS-*Sturmscharführer*		Regimental Sergeant Major	Sergeant Major
SS-*Hauptscharführer*		Sergeant Major	Master Sergeant
SS-*Oberscharführer*		(not applicable)	Technical Sergeant
SS-*Scharführer*		Colour Sergeant	Staff Sergeant
SS-*Unterscharführer*		Sergeant	Sergeant
SS-*Rottenführer*		Corporal	Corporal
SS-*Sturmmann*		Lance Corporal	(not applicable)
SS-*Oberschütze*		(not applicable)	Private 1st Class
SS-*Mann*		Private	Private

Further Reading

Agte, Patrick: *führerJochen Peiper – Commander Panzerregiment Leibstandarteführer*. 1999, J.J. Fedorowicz, Winnipeg.

Astor, Gerald: *A blood-dimmed tide*. 1992, Dell Publishing, New York.

Cavanagh, William C. C.: *A tour of the Bulge battlefield*. 2001, Pen and Sword, Barnsley.

Elstob, Peter: *Hitler's Last Offensive – The full story of the battle of the Ardennes*. 1971, Martin Secker & Warburg Limited, London.

Pallud, Jean Paul: *Battle of the Bulge then and now*. 1999, Battle of Britain International Limited, London.

Parker, Danny S.: *Battle of the Bulge – Hitler's Ardennes Offensive, 1944-1945*. 1991, Greenhill Books, London.

Pergrin, Colonel David: *Engineering the Victory – The battle of the Bulge – A history*. 1996, Schiffer Publishing Limited, Atglen, PA.

Reynolds, Michael: *The Devil's Adjutant – Jochen Peiper, Panzer Leader*. 1997, Spellmount Limited, Kent.

Reynolds, Michael: *Men of Steel – I SS Panzer Corps – The Ardennes and Eastern Front 1944-45*. 1999, Spellmount Limited, Kent.

Tiemann, Ralf: *The Leibstandarte* vol. IV/2. 1998, J.J. Fedorowicz, Winnipeg.

Toland, John: *The Battle of the Bulge*. 1998, Wordsworth Editions Limited, Hertfordshire.

INDEX